BOY SCOUTS OF AMERICA
MERIT BADGE SERIES

WHITEWATER

 BOY SCOUTS OF AMERICA®

Note to the Counselor

The instruction and experience necessary to complete the Whitewater merit badge requirements are intended to prepare the Scout for his initial whitewater experience. The objective is to introduce the skills and equipment with emphasis on safety and self-protection. A Scout earning this award will have taken the first step toward whitewater proficiency, but will achieve true proficiency only through further training and practice under proper supervision and conditions.

A Scout earning this merit badge should have a keen appreciation of the risks and precautions of whitewater sports to help ensure that future whitewater activity will be conducted in a safe manner. He must fully understand and appreciate the limits of his own ability and experience. A counselor who does not believe the Scout has reached this level of skill and understanding should not award the merit badge.

Whitewater instruction should follow all requirements, procedures, and techniques presented in this pamphlet. Supplemental information and additional strokes should not be introduced until the basic requirements are met. The learning objectives emphasize safety and basic skills proficiency. The merit badge counselor must follow all BSA safety policies, especially Safety Afloat and American Whitewater guidelines.

On-the-water instruction and practice, including the required whitewater trip, should be limited only to rapids with a rating of Class I or Class II. The minimum time for training is that which leaves the Scout prepared. The time needed for the Scout to reach adequate proficiency will vary depending on several factors, including class size and previously acquired flatwater skills. Plan on 15 to 20 hours of instruction and practice, plus the required trip. Keep the instructor-to-pupil ratio small, around 8 to 10 Scouts per pair of instructors. A recommended merit badge course outline can be found in the aquatics section of the BSA publication *Camp Program and Property Management,* No. 20-920B.

A whitewater merit badge counselor must be designated by the local council service center. Only persons trained as whitewater, canoeing, or kayaking instructors by the American Canoe Association, the American Whitewater, the U.S. Canoe Association, or by other agencies recognized by the BSA National Health and Safety Service may serve as Whitewater merit badge counselors. Persons currently trained as BSA Aquatics Instructors can assist local councils in planning for whitewater instruction and identifying counselors.

35965
ISBN 978-0-8395-3405-1
©2005 Boy Scouts of America
2010 Printing

BANG/Brainerd, MN
12-2010/060814

Requirements

1. Do the following:

    a. Review with your counselor the first aid for injuries or illnesses that could occur while working on the Whitewater merit badge, including hypothermia, heat reactions, dehydration, insect stings, blisters, bruises, cuts, and shoulder dislocation.

    b. Identify the conditions that must exist before performing cardiopulmonary resuscitation (CPR) on a person. Explain how such conditions are recognized.

    c. Demonstrate proper technique for performing CPR using a training device approved by your counselor.

2. Do the following:

    a. Review and compare BSA Safety Afloat and the American Whitewater safety guidelines and demonstrate your understanding of these principles by answering questions from your counselor.

    b. Identify and explain the use and importance of safety equipment on moving water. Include in your explanation a discussion about throw ropes, whistles, and how to choose and properly fit PFDs (personal flotation devices) and helmets.

3. Before doing requirements 4 through 13, earn the Canoeing merit badge if you will be using a canoe to earn this merit badge. If you will be using a kayak, earn the Kayaking BSA Award.

4. Do ONE of the following:

   a. If you are completing these requirements as a tandem canoeist, demonstrate basic canoe-handling skills by completing the Scout gate test within 160 seconds while paddling tandem with a buddy. Then demonstrate the following strokes: cross forward, cross draw, bow pry, Duffek, high brace, and low brace.

   b. If you are completing these requirements as a solo canoeist, demonstrate basic solo canoe-handling skills by completing the Scout gate test within 160 seconds. Then demonstrate the following strokes: cross forward, cross draw, stern pry, Duffek, high brace, and low brace.

   c. If you are using a kayak to complete these requirements, demonstrate basic kayak-handling skills by completing the Scout gate test within 160 seconds. Demonstrate the following strokes: Duffek, high brace, low brace, and sculling draw. Then do the following:

      (1) Move the kayak forward in a reasonably straight line for 10 yards.

      (2) Move the kayak sideways to the right and to the left.

      (3) Pivot 360 degrees to the right and left.

      (4) Stop the kayak.

5. Do the following:

   a. Explain the importance of scouting before committing to running a rapid, and discuss good judgment when evaluating a stretch of river or a particular rapid.

   b. Explain the terms *downstream V, riffle, strainer, eddy, eddy line, pillow, ledge, bend, shallows, falls, low-head dam, current, rock, drop, horizon line, wave, standing wave, hydraulic,* and *sleeper.*

   c. Explain how to scout and read a river while ashore and while afloat, and discuss the importance of hazard recognition.

   d. Demonstrate your ability to read the river where you are practicing and demonstrating your whitewater skills.

6. Explain the International Scale of River Difficulty and apply the scale to the stretch of river where you are practicing and demonstrating your whitewater skills. Identify the specific characteristics of the river that are factors in your classification according to the International Scale.

7. Explain the importance of communication during every whitewater outing. Explain and then demonstrate using the following river signals: "Run right," "Run left," "Run down the center," "Stop," "Are you OK?" and "Help!"

8. Do the following:

    a. Explain the differences between flatwater and whitewater canoes. Identify the different materials used in modern whitewater canoe construction and the advantages and disadvantages of each.

    b. Describe the various types of kayaks and how they differ in design, materials, and purpose.

    c. Identify the advantages and special uses for kayaks and decked canoes in moving water.

    d. Discuss the construction, safety, and functional features of paddles used in whitewater activities.

9. Discuss the personal and group equipment necessary for a safe whitewater outing and how and why it is used. Explain how to pack and protect these items.

10. Wearing the proper personal flotation device (PFD) and being appropriately dressed for the weather and water conditions, perform the following skills in moving water in a properly equipped whitewater craft of your choice (tandem canoe, solo canoe, or solo kayak). If a tandem canoe is used, the skills must be demonstrated from both the bow and stern positions.

    a. Launch and land.

    b. Paddle forward in a straight line.

    c. Backpaddle.

    d. Sideslip, both sides.

    e. Ferry upstream and downstream.

    f. Eddy turn.

    g. Peel out.

11. Explain and demonstrate:
    a. Self-rescue and procedures when capsized in moving water, including a wet exit if necessary
    b. Safe rescue of others in various whitewater situations using a throw rope
    c. Portaging—when and how to do it
    d. The whitewater buddy system using at least three persons and three craft

12. Discuss the use of inflatable rafts on moving water. In your discussion, explain the special safety precautions that should be taken when using an inflatable raft and the risks of "tubing" on moving water.

13. Participate in a whitewater trip using either a canoe or kayak on a Class I or Class II river. Help to prepare a written plan, specifying the route, schedule, equipment, safety precautions, and emergency procedures. Determine local rules and obtain permission from landowners and land managers in advance. Explain what steps you have taken to comply with BSA Safety Afloat and the American Whitewater safety guidelines. Execute the plan with others.

Contents

Safe Fun

Safe whitewater fun demands respect—respect for the river's power, your abilities, and your companions' safety. Canoeing or kayaking safely on whitewater is a matter of developing and practicing your skills and using good judgment. Have a great time and play hard, but play safe.

BSA Safety Afloat

When earning any of the aquatic merit badges, it is essential that you follow safety rules and use self-discipline and wise judgment. Tackling your first whitewater adventure will be challenging and rewarding if you understand and follow the nine points of Safety Afloat outlined below. These guidelines were developed to promote boating and boating safety and to set standards for safe unit activity afloat in flatwater or in whitewater.

1. QUALIFIED SUPERVISION

All activity afloat must be supervised by a mature and conscientious adult, age 21 or older. That person must understand and knowingly accept responsibility for the well-being and safety of those in his or her care and be trained in and committed to the nine points of Safety Afloat. The supervisor must be skilled in the safe operation of the craft for the specific activity, knowledgeable in accident prevention, and prepared for emergency situations. If the adult with Safety Afloat training lacks the necessary boat operating and safety skills, then he or she may serve as the supervisor only if assisted by other adults who have the appropriate skills.

The complete text of Safety Afloat may be found in the *Guide to Safe Scouting* on the BSA Web site: *http://www .scouting.org.*

Additional leadership is provided in ratios of one trained adult per 10 participants. At least one leader must be trained in first aid, including CPR. Any swimming done in conjunction with the activity afloat must be supervised in accordance with Safe Swim Defense standards. It is strongly recommended that all units have at least one adult or older youth member currently trained in BSA Paddle Craft Safety to assist in the planning and conduct of all activities afloat.

2. PERSONAL HEALTH REVIEW

All participants must provide evidence of a complete health history to show that they are fit for boating activities. A parent or guardian must sign health history forms for minors. Participants should relate any recent incidents of illness or injury just prior to the activity, and supervision and protection should be adjusted to anticipate any potential risks associated with individual health conditions. For significant health conditions, the adult supervisor should require an examination by a physician and consult with a parent, guardian, or caregiver for appropriate precautions.

3. SWIMMING ABILITY

For activity afloat, those not classified as a swimmer may participate on multiperson craft only on calm water where there is little likelihood of capsizing or falling overboard. They may operate a fixed-seat rowboat or pedal boat accompanied by a buddy who is a swimmer, and they may ride as a buddy in a canoe or other paddle craft with an adult swimmer skilled in that craft. They may ride as part of a group on a motorboat or sailboat operated by a skilled adult.

4. PERSONAL FLOTATION EQUIPMENT

Properly fitted U.S. Coast Guard–approved personal flotation devices (PFDs) must be worn by everyone participating in the boating activity, including rowing, canoeing, sailing, boardsailing, motorboating, waterskiing, rafting, tubing, and kayaking. Type III PFDs are recommended for general recreational use.

5. BUDDY SYSTEM

All participants in an activity afloat are paired as buddies who are always aware of each other's situation and are prepared to sound an alarm and lend assistance immediately when needed. When several craft are used on a float trip, each boat on the water should have a buddy boat. All buddy pairs must be accounted for at regular intervals during the activity and checked off the water by the qualified supervisor when the activity is over. Buddies either ride in the same boat or stay near each other when riding in single-person craft.

6. SKILL PROFICIENCY

Everyone in an activity afloat must have sufficient knowledge and skill to participate safely. Passengers should know how their movement affects boat stability and have a basic understanding of self-rescue. Boat operators must meet government requirements, be able to maintain control of their craft, know how changes in the environment influence that control, and only undertake activities within personal and group capabilities.

- Content of training exercises should be appropriate for the age, size, and experience of the participants, and should cover basic skills on calm water of limited extent before proceeding to advanced skills involving current, waves, high winds or extended distance. All instructors must have at least one assistant who can recognize and respond appropriately if the instructor's safety is compromised.

- Unit trips on whitewater above Class II must be done with either a professional guide in each craft or after all participants have received American Canoe Association or equivalent training for the class of water and type of craft involved.

7. PLANNING

Proper planning is necessary to ensure a safe, enjoyable outing. All plans should include a scheduled itinerary, notification of appropriate parties, communication arrangements, contingencies in case of bad weather or equipment failure, and emergency response options.

Preparation. Any boating activity requires access to the proper equipment and transportation of gear and participants to the site. Determine what state and local regulations are applicable. Get permission to use or cross private property. Determine whether personal resources will be used or whether outfitters will supply equipment, food, and shuttle services. Lists of group and personal equipment and supplies must be compiled and checked. Even short trips require selecting a route, checking water levels, and determining alternative pull-out locations. Changes in water level, especially on moving water, may pose significant, variable safety concerns. Obtain current charts and information about the waterway and consult those who have traveled the route recently.

Float Plan. Complete the preparation by writing a detailed itinerary, or float plan, noting put-in and pull-out locations and waypoints, along with the approximate time the group should arrive at each. Estimate your travel time generously.

Notification. File the float plan with parents, the local council office if traveling on running water, and local authorities if appropriate. Assign a member of the unit committee to alert authorities if prearranged check-ins are overdue. Make sure everyone is promptly notified when you return from the trip.

Weather. Check the forecast just before setting out, and keep an alert eye on the weather. Anticipate changes, and bring all craft ashore when rough weather threatens. Wait at least 30 minutes before resuming activities after the last incidence of thunder or lightning.

Contingencies. Planning must include identifying possible emergencies and other circumstances that could force a change of plans. Develop alternative plans for each situation. Identify local emergency resources such as EMS systems, sheriff departments, or ranger stations. Cell phones and radios can lose coverage, run out of power, or suffer water damage, so check your primary communication system and identify backups, such as the nearest residence to a campsite.

8. EQUIPMENT

All craft must be suitable for the activity, seaworthy, and float if capsized. All craft and equipment must meet regulatory standards, be properly sized, and be in good repair. Spares, repair materials, and emergency gear must be carried as appropriate. PFDs and paddles must be sized to the participants. Properly designed and fitted helmets must be worn when running rapids rated above Class II. Emergency equipment such as throw bags, signal devices, flashlights, heat sources, first-aid kits, radios, and maps must be ready for use. Spare equipment, repair materials, extra food and water, and dry clothes should be appropriate for the activity.

9. DISCIPLINE

Rules are effective only when followed. All participants should know, understand, and respect the rules and procedures for safe boating activities provided by Safety Afloat guidelines. Applicable rules should be discussed prior to the outing and reviewed for all participants near the boarding area just before the activity afloat begins. People are more likely to follow directions when they know the reasons for rules and procedures. Consistent, impartially applied rules supported by skill and good judgment provide stepping stones to a safe, enjoyable outing.

American Whitewater Safety Guidelines

Whitewater activities present new opportunities for adventure, but they also pose some additional risks that you should understand and take precautions to avoid. The following guidelines, adapted from the American Whitewater Safety Code, are geared especially for Scouting-related whitewater activities and are an excellent supplement to the Safety Afloat guidelines. Together these sets of guidelines will help ensure that your outings will be both safe and enjoyable.

1. BE A COMPETENT SWIMMER.

Being a safe whitewater boater does not require Olympian swimming skills, but you should be comfortable and competent in the water and be able to handle yourself underwater.

2. WEAR A PERSONAL FLOTATION DEVICE.

A properly fitted vest-type PFD offers back and shoulder protection as well as the flotation needed to swim safely in whitewater.

3. WEAR A SOLID, CORRECTLY FITTED HELMET.

A helmet is essential in kayaks or covered canoes and is recommended for open canoeists using thigh straps and rafters running steep drops.

4. KEEP YOUR BOAT UNDER CONTROL.

Your skills should be sufficiently developed to enable you to stop or get to shore before reaching danger. Do not enter a rapid unless you are reasonably sure that you can run it safely or swim it without injury.

5. BE AWARE OF RIVER HAZARDS.

Whitewater rivers present many hazards, such as high water or very cold water, strainers (brush or trees in the water), dams, ledges, holes, undercut rocks, or places where broaching (hitting an obstacle broadside) is likely. If you do not think you can boat around a hazard, get out and walk.

For more information about whitewater safety and to view the complete American Whitewater Safety Code, visit (with your parent's permission) *http://www.AmericanWhitewater.org.*

6. AVOID BOATING ALONE.

The recommended minimum party is three people in at least two craft.

7. KNOW THE LIMITS OF YOUR BOATING ABILITY.

Do not attempt rivers or rapids that require paddling skills more advanced than those you possess.

8. KNOW HOW TO SELF-RESCUE.

Learn and practice self-rescue techniques such as recovering from a capsize.

9. BE TRAINED IN RESCUE SKILLS.

Be able to perform CPR and first aid, including being able to recognize and treat hypothermia.

10. BE SUITABLY EQUIPPED AND PREPARED FOR EMERGENCIES.

- Wear shoes that will protect your feet.
- Carry a throw rope, knife, whistle, and waterproof matches.
- Tie your glasses on.
- Bring duct tape on short runs and a full repair kit on isolated rivers.
- Do not wear bulky clothing that could get waterlogged and hinder your ability to swim.

11. BE RESPONSIBLE FOR YOUR OWN SAFETY.

- Make thoughtful and responsible decisions about whether to participate in a trip.
- Choose appropriate equipment.
- Scout all rapids first and use your best judgment to decide whether to run or portage.
- Evaluate your own and your group's safety on an ongoing basis. Speak with anyone whose actions on the water are dangerous, whether the person is a part of your group or not.

Safety on the Water

Check over your PFD every year. Sun, sand, water, and age all take a toll on a PFD. Look for frayed fabric, broken or missing buckles, and poorly functioning zippers. Do not attempt to repair tears or rips in the material. Replace your PFD if you have any doubt about its integrity or ability to keep you afloat.

Whenever you participate in whitewater activities, you should carry adequate safety equipment and be prepared to help out in a rescue or to perform first aid. You must be aware of safety considerations at all times and be completely alert. Do not go afloat if you are fatigued. Be sure also that your whitewater partner and those in your buddy boats are fully alert, sober, and responsible.

Personal Flotation Devices and Whistles

Your PFD is your most important piece of safety equipment. If you go overboard, the support from your PFD will allow you to concentrate on righting the boat and getting back under way. In an emergency situation, it might keep an unconscious paddler afloat until help arrives. In short, wearing a properly fitted PFD helps minimize risk and saves lives.

You should wear a PFD every time you paddle, whether on a peaceful lake, a slow-moving stream, or a whitewater river. Attach a loud whistle to your PFD (using a very short cord or lanyard) so that you can sound it instantly, should you need help. Do not, however, tie it to the zipper where currents could catch it and inadvertently open your PFD.

Make sure your PFD fits correctly. To check the fit on dry land, put it on and tighten it until it is snug but not uncomfortable. Zip all zippers, buckle all buckles, tie all ties, and clinch up all side straps. Have a buddy stand behind you, grasp the material covering each shoulder, and try to pull it up straight. If the PFD can be pulled up to ear level, readjust it. You many need to try a different style or size for a better fit. The best test is to check the fit in calm water over your head. Enter the water and relax your body while tilting your head back. Your PFD should keep your chin well above the water. If it does not, readjust your PFD, try a different style (one that floats you higher in the water), or use one with a higher buoyancy rating (read the label).

U.S. Coast Guard–Approved PFDs

The following are brief descriptions of the five U.S. Coast Guard–approved PFDs. For recreational whitewater activities, Type III PFDs generally are worn.

The Type I PFD is an offshore life jacket that provides enough flotation in the chest, shoulders, and upper back areas to turn most unconscious victims faceup in rough, open water. Type I PFDs are not designed for recreational paddling, but they are suitable for passengers on cruising vessels on large bodies of water.

The Type II PFD is a near-shore buoyant vest that places all the flotation in the front and around the neck. Shaped like a horse collar and less bulky than Type I PFDs, Type II PFDs may help keep an unconscious victim faceup in calm, inland waters. It will not prevent an unconscious person from floating facedown. Type II PFDs are OK for short periods of recreational boating but are too uncomfortable to use for paddling trips.

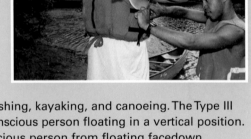

Type III PFDs most often are used for water sports such as waterskiing, fishing, kayaking, and canoeing. The Type III PFD is designed to keep a conscious person floating in a vertical position. It will not prevent an unconscious person from floating facedown. Generally, Type III PFDs have a zipper or buckle closure, and they may include adjustable side straps. They are comfortable and have a similar buoyancy as Type II PFDs.

The Type IV PFD (a circular ring, ring buoy, or seat cushion with straps used for throwing) is designed to be tossed to a person in the water. A Type IV PFD should never be used in place of a wearable PFD.

The Type V PFD is for special use only. A PFD designed for commercial whitewater rafting with extra flotation and a buoyant collar is one example of a Type V PFD. Other Type V PFDs, such as a rescue vest with a quick-release harness built into it, should be used only by someone who has had special training.

Helmets

In addition to wearing a PFD, you should always wear a helmet if you are paddling a kayak or open canoe with thigh straps (see American Whitewater safety guidelines). You should also wear a helmet in a raft when attempting a Class IV rapid, or whenever an unprotected head might put you at risk. The helmet will help protect your head in the event of a capsize or in case you need to swim in whitewater. Most helmets feature holes that allow water to drain out. When adjusting and checking fit, the helmet should feel snug but comfortable. You should be able to grasp your helmet with both hands and wiggle it a little but not enough to expose the parts of your head the helmet is intended to protect—your forehead, temples, ears, and the base of your skull.

Throw-Rope Care.
If a throw rope gets wet, hang it between two points until it is dry. Repack the rope in its bag. Store it away from heat and bright sunlight. At least once a season, inspect your throw rope inch by inch. Check that it is uncut, supple, and clean. A friend's life may depend upon it someday.

Throw Ropes

Your PFD and helmet will help keep you safe should you flip, but an accurately thrown rescue rope can quickly pull you to safety. Throw ropes are soft floating lines approximately 60 to 70 feet in length and 5/16 inch or 3/8 inch in diameter. They often are made of polypropylene, a relatively inexpensive synthetic fiber that is strong enough to haul in swimmers. Polyethylene-based rope also works very well for this purpose, although it is somewhat more costly.

Throw ropes come in a nylon bag with, typically, a disk of closed-cell foam in the bag's end. Because the ropes float, a swimmer can easily grab them. Avoid using nylon ropes because they sink and could become a potential entrapment hazard for other paddlers. (See "Rescue Techniques" for a discussion of how to use a throw rope to rescue swimmers.)

First Aid

Although there is much you can do to avoid accidents and injuries while out on the river, you should always be properly prepared to deal with them should they occur. On every river trip, carry an easily accessible waterproof first-aid kit. The longer your trip and the farther you are from civilization, the more extensive your kit should be. Always take a personal first-aid kit to cover your own needs. On group outings, a patrol first-aid kit should be sufficient. Consult the *First Aid* merit badge pamphlet or the *Fieldbook* for kit contents.

Dealing With Cold Water and Cold Weather

Hypothermia occurs when the body's core temperature falls below the normal range. Exposure to cold, or even cool, water can lower your core temperature dangerously. Early signs of heat loss include bluish lips and shivering, followed by a loss of judgment and the inability to do simple tasks. Further chilling can lead to unconsciousness and, eventually, death. Stop additional heat loss by removing the victim from the water and removing any wet clothing. Wrap warm bedding or blankets around the person and make sure to cover the head, where heat loss is the greatest. In extreme cases, keep the victim as warm as possible and call for medical aid. Before an outing, always review hypothermia treatment procedures and carry equipment for warming anyone who shows symptoms of heat loss.

Wear protective clothing (a wet or dry suit) if the water temperature is 50 degrees or less or, as a rule of thumb, if the combined water and air temperature is less than 120 degrees.

Recognizing Heat Reactions

High temperatures can pose as much of a safety threat as low temperatures. Heat reactions, including heat exhaustion and heatstroke, result when the body cannot keep itself cool enough. A person with *heat exhaustion* will have symptoms that include feeling dizzy, faint, nauseated, or weak. The victim may develop a headache or muscle cramps or look pale and be sweating heavily. Have the person lie down in a cool, shady spot with feet raised. Loosen clothing and cool the person with a damp cloth or a fan. Have the victim sip water. If the condition worsens, get medical help. Recovery should be rapid.

Heatstroke is an extreme heat reaction in which either *dehydration* (water loss) has caused body temperature to rise and sweating to stop or the body cannot lose heat fast enough and sweating occurs. The pulse is extremely rapid, and the person will be disoriented or unconscious. Cool the victim immediately through immersion or with cold packs, and increase the body's fluid level. Treat the person for shock and seek emergency help immediately. Heatstroke is a life-threatening condition.

Dehydration can occur at any temperature if a person is sweating profusely and/or not drinking enough liquids. Avoid dehydration by drinking plenty of fluids and eating enough throughout the day. If someone in your group becomes weary, confused, or develops a headache or body aches, have the person rest in the shade and sip water until the symptoms subside.

Earning the First Aid merit badge provides an excellent start in preparing for medical emergencies on land or on the water.

Sunburn is an inflammation of the skin caused by too much exposure to the sun. When sunlight reflects off the water surface, it increases the chance of being burned, so it is especially important for paddlers to cover up, use a waterproof sunscreen, and limit exposure time.

Shoulder Dislocations

Shoulder dislocations are one of the most serious injuries associated with whitewater activities. A shoulder becomes dislocated when the ball at the end of the upper arm bone slips out of the socket at the shoulder. This can happen when a paddler attempts a maneuver such as a high brace that involves reaching overhead to gain leverage with the paddle. Any stroke or maneuver in which the arm is fully extended and then rotated rearward so the elbow is behind the shoulder puts the shoulder joint in a vulnerable position. You can reduce the likelihood of such an injury by making sure you keep a slight bend in your elbows and by keeping your grip or upper hand no higher than your forehead.

If someone in your party should suffer a shoulder dislocation, put a sling on the arm and immobilize the area above and below the joint as for a collarbone fracture. Before applying the sling, place a pad between the arm and chest. Do not move the joint or attempt to put the arm bone back in the socket. Take measures to prevent the person from going into shock. Get the victim to medical attention as quickly as possible.

Minor Injuries

Paddlers can get insect bites or stings while afloat or when preparing to launch from the shore. The best strategies for avoiding stings and bites are to use insect repellent and wear long-sleeved shirts and long pants when in buggy areas. For typical insect stings and bites, apply first aid as described in your *Boy Scout Handbook*. For severe and prolonged pain, or any severe reaction, dizziness, or respiratory distress, get medical help.

Bruises are injuries that cause bleeding under the skin. Applying an ice pack to a bruise will reduce pain and swelling. Minor wounds, such as cuts, should be washed carefully with soap and water and covered with a sterile bandage or dressing to prevent infection. Deeper cuts or puncture wounds may need stitches, antibiotics, and a tetanus shot to prevent infection. For these injuries, visit a doctor as soon as possible.

Blisters form when skin is irritated, usually by friction or heat. A hot spot signals the beginning of a blister. Stop immediately and protect the tender area by cutting a piece of moleskin or molefoam and covering the affected area. If a blister forms, build up several layers of moleskin or molefoam, as needed, to take off the pressure. Blisters are best left unbroken. Treat a broken blister as you would a minor cut.

Cardiopulmonary Resuscitation

Cardiopulmonary resuscitation (CPR) is a procedure used on someone whose breathing and heartbeat have stopped. It is only for extreme emergencies. CPR is required only when someone has no pulse, indicating that the heart has stopped beating. Someone's heart may stop in the event of a heart attack or drowning. CPR includes both chest compressions and rescue breathing (mouth-to-mouth resuscitation). The procedure provides the blood circulation and breathing that could save the victim's life. CPR should not be performed on someone who has a pulse but is simply unconscious. A drowning victim may stop breathing but could still have a pulse. In this case, rescue breathing, not CPR, is the correct procedure to follow.

A frightened or anxious victim might breathe too heavily or too deeply, which can result in hyperventilation. Calmly encourage the person to relax and breathe slowly.

CPR courses are designed to teach rescuers how to recognize life-threatening conditions and respond appropriately. Check with the American Red Cross, the American Heart Association, and other similar organizations in your area to find out if they offer CPR and other first-aid training. Every river trip should include one or more persons with current CPR training. You need to know CPR before you have to use it.

Reading a River

Before you set foot in your boat, take the time to learn as much as you can about the stretch of river you will be running. Find out about the river's unique features and hazards and identify what class of rapids you will be dealing with. If possible, scout your route to avoid unpleasant and potentially dangerous surprises.

When scouting a river, be sure to wear your helmet.

River Features

The term *whitewater* refers to a stretch of swiftly moving water that becomes white and foamy as it passes over or around obstacles. A *rapid* is a turbulent, fast-flowing stretch of river that contains obstructions above or below the water. Rapids may feature *drops* in which the water abruptly descends over rocks or a ledge.

Current describes the continuous movement of water in a certain direction. The strength of the current is affected by three things: gradient, flow, and depth. The steeper the gradient (or slope of riverbed) and the higher the volume of flow, the more powerful the current.

Water in a river flows in different layers at different speeds. In straight channels, the layers just beneath the surface and in the middle of the river flow faster than the layers on the bottom or on the sides because there is less friction with the air than there is with the river bottom or banks. As the riverbed widens and the water becomes less deep, the current slows and *shallows* (shallow areas) develop.

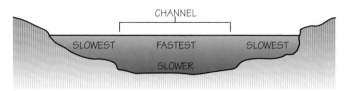

Speed of currents in a straight river

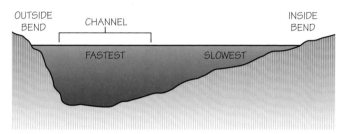

Speed of currents in a river bend

The amount of water flowing downstream changes seasonally, daily, and sometimes hourly. A river's flow is measured in cubic feet per second (CFS).

When a river turns, it forms a *bend*. The strongest, deepest, and fastest current will usually be found on the outside of bends. You usually will find the biggest waves on the outside of the curve, and the smallest waves, called *riffles*, running on the inside. Here the water is the slowest as it passes over sand or gravel bars.

The beds of most whitewater rivers are littered with rocks, but when a paddler talks about *rocks*, he or she usually is referring to rocks jutting above the river's surface. Logs and trees just below the surface are called *sleepers*.

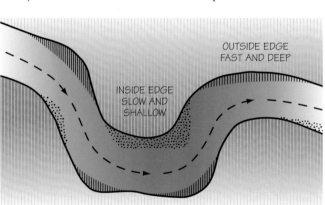

Ledges are rock shelves that extend from the bank into the river or are submerged. A series of ledges can form a stair-step rapid. Big ledges can create *falls,* or a drop where water free-falls at least part of the way. Ledges usually warrant a look-see before running.

A *downstream* **V** forms when current flows between two obstructions, such as midstream rocks or the walls of a narrow canyon. A downstream V's wide end faces upstream and its apex, or narrow end, faces downstream. Steep diagonal waves usually define the sides of the V, forcing boaters to the middle of the V, where the fastest current and deepest water are found. Running the downstream V can be the easiest route through a rapid, but huge waves can form at the bottom of the V. These waves can fill a canoe with water or flip a boat. Canoes with flotation bags can minimize the amount of water sloshing about in the boat.

As you paddle downstream, you will often see a *pillow*—a layer of slack water that cushions the upstream face of a rock as the river pours over.

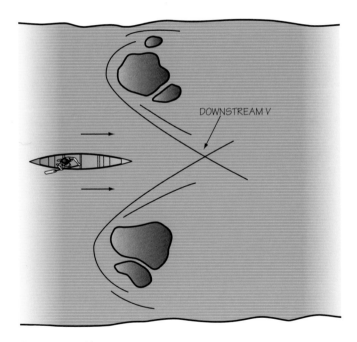

Downstream V

To tell the difference between eddies and holes, remember this: Water flows into eddies and then out again at the surface. Water flows into holes, recirculates for a while, then flows out along the river bottom.

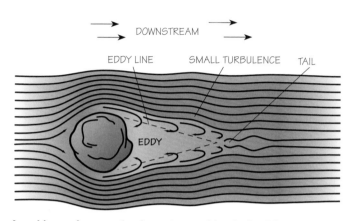

DOWNSTREAM

EDDY LINE   SMALL TURBULENCE   TAIL

EDDY

An eddy can form on the downstream side of a boulder.

Eddies are relatively calm waters where the main current reverses its flow. They are found downstream of rocks, bridge pilings, jutting cliff faces, and so forth. As the current flows around a rock or other natural or artificial structure, it parts left and right, leaving a hollow area immediately behind the rock. The water behind the obstacle is lower than the water on either side, so water flows back upstream to fill the hole, running counter to the river's main current. Eddies may be several hundred feet across behind a point of land or as small as a dinner plate behind a rock.

Shallow currents flow over an obstacle to create a hole on the downstream side.

Eddy lines are the often-visible lines where the downstream current rubs up against an eddy's upstream current. This forms a ridge in the water that tapers from high to low the farther downstream you move in the eddy.

Holes are areas behind obstacles where a trough forms, followed by a wave that curls back toward the hole. *Recirculating holes* are extremely dangerous holes that form over an obstruction or following a sudden drop in the riverbed, with most of their water recirculating instead of flowing back into the river downstream of the obstruction. In a recirculating hole, water flows in from all sides and flows out along the river bottom. Recirculating holes usually feature violent, aerated water and powerful tumbling current.

Waves are stationary ridges of water. Sometimes at the bottom of a rapid, waves form a series of standing waves called a *wave train*. This line of waves forms, one wave following another and gradually decreasing in size, until the falling water dissipates its energy.

Standing waves can be fun to ride. You will feel as if the river is standing still and your boat is being raised and lowered like a yo-yo. At other times, standing waves can be steep enough to overturn or fill boats.

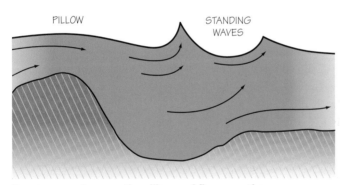

PILLOW

STANDING WAVES

Deeper currents cover the pillow and flow over the obstacle to form standing waves farther downstream.

River Hazards

Recirculating holes and riverwide waves can be created by artificial structures such as weirs or low-head dams. *Low-head dams* (usually made of concrete or rock rubble) often stretch from bank to bank, typically without a break for the current to flow through. Instead, the river falls evenly over the structure, forming an often lethal, unbroken wave.

Never run drops formed by low-head dams or weirs. They are aptly called "drowning machines." Their symmetry forms a very dangerous recirculating hole with no defined downstream flow and no opportunity to escape downstream or to the side. Many times they are marked on maps. Identify each one during trip planning and make sure each can be and is safely portaged.

Also be on the lookout when you are out on the water for low-head dams or waterfalls that are not marked on maps. They often give themselves away by revealing an unbroken horizon line. A *horizon line* is formed when the river steepens and the rapid or falls formed by this sudden drop is below your sight line, thus marking a steep drop, a falls, or a low-head dam. Always stop and scout drops with horizon lines. Horizon lines frequently indicate a mandatory portage.

If you find your boat going sideways down the river and you are approaching an obstacle like a large rock in this position, try to avoid *broaching*. Broaching occurs when your boat is sideways to the current and gets pushed up against an obstacle. Broaching can be dangerous, especially for beginners, and is best avoided. *Vertical pinning* occurs when the boat goes over a steep drop and the bow sticks in the river bed below, usually jammed between rocks.

If you begin to broach, lean toward the obstacle and allow the current to flow underneath and around the hull. If you lean upstream, away from the obstacle, the current will usually flip

HORIZON LINE

Horizon lines appear as an unbroken line, often stretching from bank to bank. You will see the river running up to this line, then disappearing, to become visible a distance downstream.

Avoid getting any part of your body between your boat and an obstacle if your boat broaches. Not only can the current's force wrap boats, but it can entrap paddlers, sometimes with fatal consequences.

Broaching

the boat upstream. If you are in a canoe, the water will fill the boat like a big tub. If you are in a kayak, water will tend to push the boat down, deeper into the water, entrapping you inside. If it looks like you are going to pin, get out of your boat—fast—and onto the obstacle.

The best way to avoid broaching is to keep the boat pointed downstream. It is better to hit a rock straight on with the bow than to try to turn in the current and end up going sideways.

Undercut rocks are rocks that have been eroded under water. They often are invisible from the surface and can entrap boats. They are very dangerous and can be fatal. Avoid undercut rocks by boating or portaging around drops with undercut rocks.

Strainers are obstacles that come in many guises but always spell big trouble. Tree limbs (also called *sweepers)* are a common type of strainer. They comb the current—stopping boats and boaters while allowing the current to flow cleanly through. Downed trees or roots also snare unwary boaters. Artificial strainers such as fencing, old cables or pipes, and chunks of concrete and rebar form severe hazards on some rivers. Portage around any strainer that you are not confident you can safely pass.

Low-hanging tree branches often create strainers.

When in Doubt, Scout!

The time of year, fallen trees, and rainfall are just several elements that can transform a normally safe route into a dangerous one. Always scout ahead, plan your run, and identify several options in case your run does not go as planned.

Before running a section of whitewater, a blind corner, or a potential drop of any sort, land your boat and scout ahead along the shore to make sure that there are no upcoming obstacles that might be beyond your ability to navigate.

When scouting a river, it is important that everyone use the same terms to describe what they see. *Downstream* describes the direction in which the current is flowing toward the mouth of the river, and *upstream* describes the direction opposite the general flow of the current. *River right* and *river left* always refer to the right side or the left side of the river as if you were facing downstream.

Scouting ahead helps you choose the safest route through rough water. Start planning your run at the downstream end and work your way back upstream. First know where you want to end up, then figure out *if* and *how* you can get there safely. Look things over to identify hazards, and discuss them with your buddies.

Note landmarks that might help you know when to begin that critical midrapid move. While walking back to your boat, stop several times to squat down and look back downstream. Try to imagine how things will look from water level. Break your run into sections. By doing so, you can break down an imposing stretch of foam and spray into a series of planned maneuvers. Identify several options to use in case your run does not go according to your original plan.

Rivers change from one day to the next. You need to know what is around the next bend or over the next drop. Normal erosion, floods, fallen trees, and new fences may transform overnight a safe route into a hazardous one. Remember that water levels rise and fall with the seasons and after rains. Sudden dam releases may lower or raise water levels drastically, dramatically changing a river's character. Don't take anything for granted.

International Scale of River Difficulty

The International Scale of River Difficulty provides a standard-ized classification system for rating the difficulty and risks in running rapids. River runners use the scale as a rough but use-ful means of comparing the difficulty of one river with another. As a beginner, your paddling will be in Class I and Class II whitewater so that you can build skills in water where you can have fun with relatively low risk. In addition, you can develop new skills safely by practicing difficult moves in easy rapids.

The scale (from Class I through the extreme Class VI) is useful only if you understand your own capabilities and limita-tions and those of your companions. Although Class I and II rapids are good choices for beginners, you may find yourself deciding to run a rapid you portaged last time or portaging a rapid you ran previously. For instance, cold or high water can raise a rapid's difficulty by one or more levels.

In addition, you should consider a river's rating to be one class higher if the sum of the temperature of the water and air totals less than 120 degrees or if the trip is on a remote river. As you gain experience, you will learn to exercise progressively sophisticated judgment about both the river and yourself. Always choose safety and common sense when in doubt.

International Scale of River Difficulty

Here are the six classifications used for the International Scale of River Difficulty.

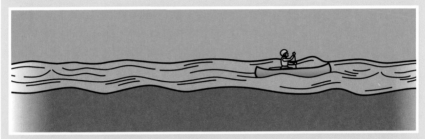

Class I: Fast-moving water with riffles and small waves. Few or no obstructions. Risk to swimmers is slight; self-rescue is easy.

Class II: Straightforward rapids with wide, clear channels. Some maneuvering may be required, but rocks and medium-size waves are easily avoided by trained paddlers. Swimmers are seldom at risk.

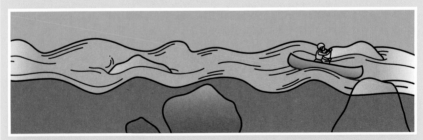

Class III: Rapids with moderate, irregular waves that may swamp an open canoe. Complex maneuvering is often required. Some risk to swimmers; group assistance may be necessary.

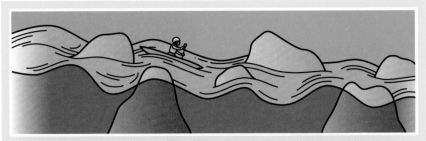

Class IV: Powerful, but predictable, rapids requiring precise boat handling in turbulent water. May feature large, unavoidable waves and holes or narrow passages demanding fast maneuvers. Risk to swimmers is moderate to high; self-rescue may be difficult and group assistance is often necessary.

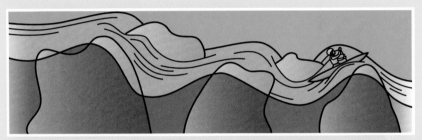

Class V: Extremely long, obstructed, or very violent rapids. Drops may feature large, unavoidable waves and holes or steep, congested chutes with complex, demanding routes. Eddies may be turbulent or difficult to reach. Swims are dangerous, and rescue is often difficult, even for experts.

Class VI: These runs have almost never been attempted because they are extremely difficult, unpredictable, and dangerous. The consequences of errors are very severe and rescue may be impossible. Only teams of experts who have taken every precaution should attempt them, and only when water levels are favorable.

Boats, Paddles, and Other Equipment

Canoes and kayaks designed for whitewater are more sturdily built than those designed for flatwater. They are designed to bounce or slide off rocks, to turn quickly, and to be forgiving in turbulent water.

Boat Materials

Most whitewater canoes and kayaks are made of plastic, plastic-foam composites, or Kevlar® and carbon-fiber composites. Aluminum canoes and fiberglass canoes and kayaks were once the most popular boats for whitewater. They have been replaced by modern plastic boats but still remain very common for trips on moving water without rapids. Each material has advantages and disadvantages. When selecting a boat, you will need to consider expense, your skill level, and how well the boat material will stand up to the type of river running you will be doing.

Decked Canoes

Solo and tandem covered canoes, called C-1s and C-2s, are a treat to watch as they run heavy white water or slip through slalom gates. Like kayaks, paddlers in C-boats are decked, so paddlers wear spray skirts that allow them to stay dry in big waves and to play in holes. C-boat paddlers kneel on a pedestal rather than sit in a seat, and they use a single paddle.

The table here lists some common canoe and kayak materials and lists the advantages and disadvantages of each.

Whitewater Canoe and Kayak Materials

Material	Advantages	Disadvantages
ABS Royalex™ (acrylonitrile butadiene styrene), cross-linked vinyl, ABS plastic, and ABS closed-cell foam sandwiched together	Strong; flexes instead of breaks; quiet, repairable, moderately priced; the most common material used to build whitewater canoes	Heavy; dents and scratches easily; sometimes too flexible; cannot be shaped into fine bows and sterns; repairs can be difficult; heavier than fiberglass or Kevlar®
Polyethylene (plastic or plastic and foam, injected or molded in a form)	Flexes instead of breaks; quiet; least expensive; the most common material used to build kayaks	Very difficult to outfit and repair; sometimes too flexible; often very heavy
Aluminum	Strong and weatherproof; less expensive than some materials	Noisy; "sticks" to rocks; not lightweight; cannot be shaped into fine bows and sterns; external keel ill-suited for whitewater; more difficult to outfit; heavier than fiberglass
Fiberglass	Strong; lighter than ABS; can be formed into sophisticated shapes; stiff; easier to outfit and repair; moderately priced	Less durable than ABS; heavier than Kevlar®; few whitewater-specific canoes and kayaks are made of fiberglass
Kevlar®/carbon fiber	Very strong for its weight; can be formed into sophisticated shapes; very stiff; relatively easy to outfit and repair; often used for competition and elite whitewater canoes and kayaks	Most expensive; less tolerant of abuse than ABS

Differences in Whitewater and Flatwater Canoe Design

Whitewater solo canoes vary from 11 to 14 feet in length, and are usually less than 30 inches wide. Tandem whitewater canoes are 14 to 16 feet long and 32 to 36 inches wide. The average whitewater canoe's bow and stern are fuller than those designed for flatwater or ocean touring. This aids buoyancy and reduces the chance that the ends of the boat will get buried in a wave.

Whitewater canoes are built with more rocker than flatwater boats. *Rocker* is the term used to describe a boat's end-to-end profile. The bottom of the boat curves up, like a banana, toward the front and back of the boat. This shape helps whitewater canoes turn quickly. Flatwater boats have much less rocker, which helps them track in a straight line.

Another way whitewater canoes differ from flatwater canoes is that they often have higher sides to help keep out waves. Some whitewater canoes are designed with *tumblehome*, an inward curving of the upper section of the side of the canoe. On well-designed whitewater boats, tumblehome does not adversely affect the boat's stability and makes it considerably easier to paddle because the hand on the paddle shaft can be kept closer to the boat.

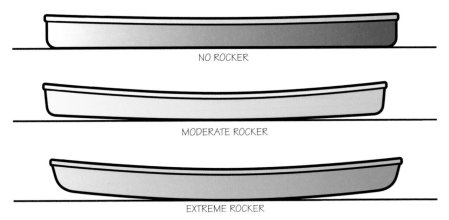

NO ROCKER

MODERATE ROCKER

EXTREME ROCKER

Canoe rocker

Types of Kayaks

Install extra flotation (air bags or plastic foam) in your whitewater boat to ensure your boat will ride high in the water if you flip.

Most modern kayaks are made of rigid plastics such as polyethylene, fiberglass, or Kevlar®. Kayak designs vary according to usage and construction. For example, a flatwater racer differs from a whitewater racer. Recreational kayaks are multipurpose craft suitable for a variety of water conditions. Touring kayaks are larger and have storage capacity for camping gear. They are also known as sea kayaks, due to their use around ocean shorelines. These kayaks are built long—up to 20 feet— to aid in tracking, and they often have a rudder, or *skeg*. Sit-on-top kayaks do away with the traditional cockpit and deck in favor of a recessed well that is self-bailing. Inflatable kayaks are made of the same materials as whitewater rafts and are very stable. Inflatables are open, like rafts, with the paddler sitting on the floor of the boat.

Special play boats, also called *rodeo kayaks,* are used in heavy whitewater. Some play boat designs are adapted for surfing. They are only 6 to 9 feet long and 2 feet wide, with low decks and hard chines (where the floor meets the sides). Short boats are slow boats, but what they sacrifice in speed they gain in maneuverability. Low decks make it easier to play in holes; flat bottoms make it easier to spin; and hard chines make carving turns and steering easier.

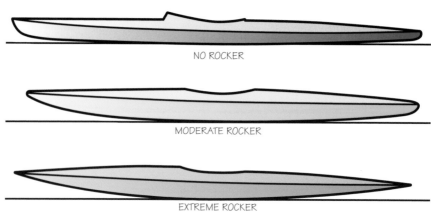

NO ROCKER

MODERATE ROCKER

EXTREME ROCKER

Kayak rocker

Paddles

On every trip, you will lift your paddle thousands of times, making a lightweight but sturdy paddle worth its weight in gold. The best paddle shafts are *indexed,* or oval, not round. An indexed shaft helps you control the boat and is easy on your hands. Paddle blade shape is important as well. The best whitewater paddles combine lightweight strength with shapes that "stick" in the water, then move cleanly through the water.

Whitewater canoe paddles are made of wood, aluminum, plastic, and composite materials, such as fiberglass, Kevlar®, and carbon fiber. Most whitewater canoe paddles feature a T-grip for better feedback and control. Blades vary in size, but most have a medium-size blade that is steady and predictable in the water. The tip of the blade is often constructed with an insert of a durable material such as aluminum or polyurethane.

Kayak paddles have blades at both ends. Usually the blades are set at an angle to each other from 45 to 90 degrees. The offset angle allows the paddle blade out of the water to be automatically feathered. Feathering reduces the effect of wind and wave on the blade. Shafts are indexed and blades are oriented so that either your left or right hand is the control hand. Your control hand constantly grips the shaft while your noncontrol hand allows the paddle to swivel and feather between strokes. Some kayak paddles break into two shorter pieces for storage and transport.

Kayak blades in profile can be either flat or curved and either a simple oval or a complex curved shape. Kayak paddle faces can be flat or hollowed. Whitewater kayak paddles are shorter and generally more symmetrical than touring kayak paddles.

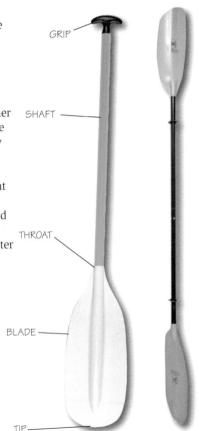

GRIP

SHAFT

THROAT

BLADE

TIP

Whitewater Rafts

Rafts are inflated watercraft that come in a variety of shapes and sizes. Paddle rafts are paddled by a crew of paddlers, while oar rafts are rowed by a single oarsperson. Most rafts are 10 to 16 feet long and oval. The hulls are made of inflatable

Outfitting

Most whitewater canoes and kayaks feature special outfitting to hold paddlers securely in their boats. Foot braces, for example, help both kayakers and canoeists hold themselves in their boats with their legs and knees. Releasable thigh straps keep canoeists from falling out when the boat is tipped or upside down.

In addition, most whitewater canoes are outfitted with rigid foam or plastic pedestals (or "saddles") on which paddlers kneel astride. Pedestals offer much better control over a canoe and, by virtue of being easier to tumble off of than bench seats, are safer in the event of a capsize. Knee pads glued into a canoe keep paddlers from sliding around and ease the discomfort of kneeling.

Kayakers pad their boat's cockpit so that it will fit like a glove for the purpose of control while on moving water. Most whitewater kayaks include pillars or bulkheads made of foam to keep their decks from collapsing should they broach. Pillars, usually placed fore and aft, brace the floor and deck between kayakers' legs or in front of their feet and behind their boat's seat.

All canoe and kayak outfitting must be installed with safety in mind. Most outfitting is glued into boats with adhesives specifically designed for the task; **many are toxic.** For this reason, find a qualified outfitter who is an experienced whitewater paddler to help you make sure your outfitting is functional, properly installed, and safe to use.

tubes about 14 to 20 inches in diameter. These tubes are made of sturdy synthetic rubber or vinyl. Oared rafts are coupled to an aluminum frame that holds gear, seats, and rowlocks. Most modern whitewater rafts are self-bailing, that is, they feature an inflated floor with drain holes that allow water to flow out of the boat.

The size and weight of a whitewater raft make it a stable and forgiving craft that is ideal for carrying gear. Because whitewater rafts are big and heavy, they are slower and less agile than are canoes or kayaks when it comes to catching eddies, surfing, and playing in rapids.

Tubing

Tubing can be loads of fun, but there are many hazards to consider. Inner tubes are difficult to steer and they offer almost no protection in a collision. In addition, their inflation valves and stems tend to cut and scratch their riders. When tied together, tubes become a significant entrapment hazard. This is why you should only go tubing on slow-moving water. You must wear shoes and your PFD. Take a buddy, and make sure you follow the BSA Safety Afloat guidelines.

Every kayaking party should have at least one spare paddle; every canoe should have one, too. Canoeists' spare paddles should be securely fastened to their boats, out of the way, but readily at hand in case they are needed.

Rafting Safety

Whitewater safety precautions for canoeing and kayaking apply to rafting, too. If you are in a paddle raft, always wear a PFD and follow the other BSA Safety Afloat guidelines.

Rafting injuries are frequently caused by paddle contact. Remember that you are riding beside another paddler, and there is another person paddling close behind or in front of you. Keep the blade on the outside of the craft, and grip the paddle low and close to your own body. If you capsize or fall overboard while rafting, reach out to the side, grasp the grab line, pull yourself out from under the raft, and move to the upstream end.

Do not overlook the safety of others on the river. A six-person raft plowing through the rapids can run over a kayak like a bus running over a bicycle. Look ahead and be sure the rapids are clear when you begin your run.

Basic Whitewater Skills

If you are itching to become a great paddler, you need to practice to perfect basic strokes and form so that you will have the confidence and skill to meet the challenges of whitewater paddling.

Body Mechanics and Position

It is important to be mindful of body mechanics and form whether you are on flatwater or whitewater. Proper form will keep you safer and ensure that you get the most out of the effort you expend.

Always grip your paddle with your hands a little more than shoulder-width apart and your paddle shaft perpendicular to the water. Canoeists should keep one hand on their paddle's grip. When performing strokes like the cross draw, avoid letting your upper paddle hand rise above your head—if your paddle is yanked backward in strong current or if it strikes a rock, you are vulnerable to dislocating your shoulder.

When paddling in a solo canoe or kayak, you are, of course, solely responsible for powering and steering. Keep your eyes on your target and make lots of small corrections. Little corrections are easy and keep you moving along; big corrections are harder and slow you down.

Tandem canoeists paddle on opposite sides. This helps move the canoe in a straight line and provides tremendous stability. The bow paddler provides power, initiates many maneuvers, and provides stability. The stern paddler steers the canoe with a combination of power and steering strokes.

On flatwater, the bow paddler usually follows the stern paddler's lead. On whitewater, however, the bow paddler might have a clearer view of the river and so may direct the boat's path on the water. The best whitewater paddlers constantly communicate about where they want to go on the river.

Most of your paddling power comes from your torso—from coiling and uncoiling the large muscles of your back, stomach, and shoulders.

In a tandem canoe, the stern paddler's forward strokes will have more effect on the canoe's direction than will those of the bow paddler, and will usually cause the boat to turn away from the stern paddler's selected paddling side. The same is true when paddling solo: The forward stroke commonly turns the canoe to the paddler's offside. Efficient stern and solo paddling include a steering component at the end of each stroke. There are many different steering strokes (J-stroke, C-stroke, Canadian stroke), but to begin with, canoeists should focus on developing a dependable J-stroke.

> Canoe paddling positions are termed *onside* and *offside*. For solo canoeists, the side on which the paddler performs the forward stroke is the onside position. The opposite side becomes the offside. In tandem canoes, the side on which the bow paddler does the forward stroke becomes the onside.

Recall that all strokes can be divided into the following three phases:

- **Catch**—In this position, the paddle blade has entered the water and the paddle shaft is perpendicular. The force of the blade applied by the paddler against the water is now equal to the water's resistance. The paddler feels the paddle "grab" the water.

- **Power**—The torso uncoils, delivering the power of the muscles of the upper body to the blade through the shaft.

- **Recovery**—The stroke has ended and now the blade is lifted out of the water, and set up for another stroke in the catch position.

Scout Gate Test

To make sure you have mastered the basic canoeing and kayaking skills you learned while earning your Canoeing merit badge or Kayaking BSA Award, you need to complete the Scout gate test within 160 seconds. To prepare for the test, you may want to review and practice strokes such as the forward stroke, backstroke, draw stroke, pushaway stroke, forward sweep, reverse sweep, and J-stroke.

The Scout gate test is a variation of a classic canoe and kayak training drill used by slalom paddlers to build strength, speed, and technique. The test is conducted on flatwater using floats, floats supporting upright poles, or poles hanging above the water. If you use floats, anchor each float separately and use a 4-foot spreader about 20 inches under the water to keep the floats apart. If the poles are suspended above the water, position them 4 feet apart and about 2 inches above the surface.

Your ready position for the first pass should be in front of the gate, with your bow just outside the gate.

The five gate passes for the Scout gate test are as follows:

1. On the "go" signal, paddle through the gate; pivot right 180 degrees after the boat's stern has cleared the gate.

2. Return through the gate paddling forward; now pivot left 180 degrees.

3. Return a third time through the gate, paddling forward, then sideslip right.

4. Back up outside of the right pole (or float) and go forward through the gate.

5. Back up outside of the left pole, and go forward through the gate for your fifth and final time. Your time ends when the stern of your boat clears the gate.

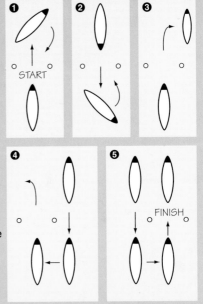

Hints:

- Stay close to the gates while turning and reversing direction.

- Practice by paddling slowly, but smoothly, through the gates. Build speed over time.

- Try different stroke combinations and determine which ones work best for you.

- Avoid touching the gates. Each time you touch the gate pole or float with your boat, paddle, or body, 5 penalty seconds are added to your time.

Whitewater Paddle Strokes

Practice whitewater paddle strokes and maneuvers on flatwater or on a slow-moving river. Practice slowly, working first toward precision and later adding power and speed.

The Cross Forward—Canoe

A cross stroke is any stroke performed on the paddler's offside without switching hands. The *cross forward stroke* is a forward stroke done on the offside. It is frequently used by solo canoeists to keep the boat moving forward while correcting the tendency of the bow to go to the offside. The cross forward brings the bow back to the onside.

- **Catch**—Without switching hands, swing your paddle across your boat. Twist your upper body, rotating your shaft-hand shoulder forward and your grip-hand shoulder backward. Lean forward about 45 degrees, and place your blade (buried to its throat) at the ready in the water. Your grip-hand elbow will be behind your head (at about ear level), and your arms should be extended out in front of you.

- **Power**—Forcefully bring your torso to an upright, vertical position while pulling your hips toward your paddle. Your paddle should stay perpendicular to the water.

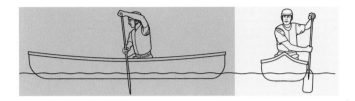

- **Recovery**—When your blade reaches your hips, rotate your grip-hand thumb forward so that your paddle's leading edge is parallel to your boat. Slice your paddle through the water back to the catch position. Rotate the blade so that it is ready for your next stroke.

Draws

When you earned the Canoeing merit badge or the Kayaking BSA Award, you learned to do the basic *draw stroke* to move your boat sideways toward the paddle. Whitewater boating uses several variations of the draw stroke.

Canoeists use the *stationary draw* to harness the river's power to pull the boat toward the paddle. This is an especially useful stroke for entering and leaving eddies. To execute a stationary draw from an eddy, move to the catch position with your paddle shaft vertical in the water and your blade buried to its throat. The paddle of the bow paddler or solo canoeist should be planted in the downstream current just outside the eddy line. Do not pull the boat toward the paddle. Instead, slightly tilt the up-current edge of your paddle away from your boat and hold it there. The current will grab your paddle and "fly" it; all you have to do is hang on.

Sculling draw

Both canoeists and kayakers can use the *sculling draw* to pull the boat sideways or initiate a turn. Hold the paddle with your upper or grip hand no higher than your forehead and your other hand positioned about a shoulder-width lower on the paddle shaft. The paddle shaft should be vertical and move in a path 2 to 3 feet long next to the side of the boat. Angle the blade at 45 degrees—as if you were spreading butter on a slice of bread—and move the paddle from side to side. At the end of each stroke, move the blade back in the opposite direction with the forward edge up. In the sculling draw, the paddle strokes the shape of an infinity sign (a sideways figure eight) in the water.

The bow paddler or solo canoe paddler also uses a *cross draw* to move the boat sideways or initiate a turn. Without switching hands, set up a cross draw by rotating your torso perpendicular to the keel line of the canoe.

The elbow of your grip-hand arm should be well below the level of your shoulder and rotated behind you. Your blade goes into the water with your torso still coiled.

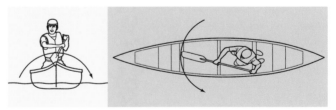

Setting up a cross draw

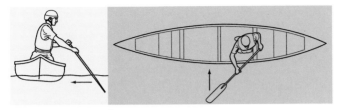

Cross draw power phase

The power phase is simple—just leave your arms and hands pretty much where they are, and unwind your upper body, drawing the boat toward your paddle's blade. Be sure you do not allow the blade under your boat. The cross draw is such a powerful stroke that you can tip your boat if you do not stop in time.

Recover by dropping your grip hand. Re-rotate and twist your torso, place the paddle back in the water, and repeat

Pries

The *pry* stroke complements the draw. The draw moves the boat toward your paddle; the pry moves it away. The *bow pry* and *stern pry* are used by canoeists but rarely by kayakers. Instead of doing a pry stroke on one side of the boat, the kayaker can simply do a draw stroke on the other side to get the same results. Pries are powerful strokes for moving a canoe toward the paddler's offside.

- **Catch**—For the bow pry, hold your paddle perpendicular to the canoe's keel line, then place your paddle in the water with its blade buried to the throat. Keep your forearm in front of your face and your hand that is on the grip farther out over the water than your lower hand. This will position the blade slightly underneath the bow. Your lower hand must be above the gunwales or your paddle shaft must be between your hand (particularly your thumb) and the gunwales. The pry often uses the gunwales as a fulcrum, so be careful not to pinch your thumb between your paddle and the gunwales.

    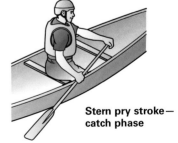

    Stern pry stroke— catch phase

    For the stern pry, hold the paddle shaft parallel to the side of the boat and place the grip end of your paddle out over the water. Put the blade in the water to the throat so that the blade is slightly underneath the stern. The shaft hand should hold the shaft against the gunwales.

From the stern of a solo or tandem canoe, the stern pry is a powerful turning or correction stroke. Keep the pry stroke short and fast. Repeat the stroke if necessary.

- **Power**—Use the gunwales as a fulcrum and pull your grip hand into the boat. The power of the stroke increases with the speed you move your grip hand. Keep the stroke short—about a foot or so—since the blade quickly begins pulling your gunwales down, rather than pushing them away.

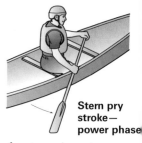

Stern pry stroke— power phase

- **Recovery**—You can do either an out-of-water or in-water recovery. The out-of-water recovery is more efficient for the stern pry and requires that you drop your grip hand down toward your lap, slicing the blade out of the water. Return to the starting point of the stroke by moving the grip hand out over the water and the blade underneath the stern. The in-water recovery is more efficient for the bow pry. At the end of the stroke, turn the thumb of the grip hand away from you and then slice the blade back underneath the bow as you move the grip hand back out over the water.

Pry stroke for canoe

The pry stroke will move your canoe away from the paddling side. Holding the paddle as you would for a draw stroke, slip the blade back into the water next to the canoe and pry it away. Though it can be hard on the paddle loom, you can brace the loom against the canoe, using the gunwale as a fulcrum or pivot for leveraging the stern away from the blade of the paddle.

Duffek

The Duffek is named after the innovative Czech kayaker Milovan Duffek. The Duffek stroke is a static stroke. The paddler plants the paddle near the bow and lets the momentum of the boat or current push the other end of the canoe or kayak around it. When the paddle is placed in the water, the thumb of the grip hand points in toward the boat. This turns the forward edge of the blade away from the boat, causing the paddle to act as a pivot point with the boat swinging around it.

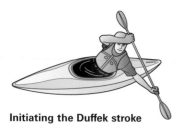

Initiating the Duffek stroke

Some people refer to a certain combination of strokes as the Duffek, but a more appropriate name is the Duffek maneuver. This maneuver combines a Duffek stroke with a draw to the bow, followed by a forward stroke. The cross Duffek maneuver begins with a cross Duffek (a Duffek done on the offside without switching hands) followed by a cross draw to the bow and ending with a cross forward stroke. The Duffek and Duffek maneuver are primarily used to enter and leave eddies. Practice the Duffek in flatwater using a buoy and a little forward speed.

Braces

Braces are intended to catch you if you start to tip. The *low brace* is a stabilizing stroke that prevents you from tipping over. You can do a low brace upstream or downstream from your boat. In a canoe, you execute the low brace when your boat starts tipping toward your onside. In a kayak, you can use the low brace for either side.

Low brace for canoe

In a solo canoe or kayak, execute a low brace by quickly placing your paddle flat on the water (perpendicular to the length of your boat). Press the paddle firmly down on the water and use your knees and torso to flatten out your boat. The low brace is the preferred stroke to prevent onside capsizing.

A *high brace* is a stroke that is used to prevent tipping to the paddler's offside. As the boat tips away from the paddler's onside, the paddler reaches out and does a quick draw stroke to right the boat. This stroke is usually less effective than the low brace, but in solo canoes, it is the only possible stroke to do if your boat is tipping away from the side you are paddling on.

Low brace for kayak

Paddlers in tandem canoes must learn to do a combination of braces to prevent the boat from tipping over. If the boat tips to the onside (the bow paddler's paddling side), the bow paddler would do a low brace while the stern paddler would do a high brace. If the boat tips to the offside, the bow paddler would do a high brace while the stern paddler would do a low brace.

High brace for kayak

Whitewater Maneuvers

Savvy boaters use the river's power to take them where they want to go. Technique, not strength, is what you need to control your boat on the river.

Launching and Landing

You are as likely to upset your boat launching and landing as you are when on moving water. If you are using a canoe, enter and exit only when your boat is completely in the water. Launch and land with your canoe parallel to the shore so that the boat is fully afloat and you can step in or out without clambering over your load.

As you step into or climb out of your canoe, keep three points of contact with the boat. Step into the center of your boat, keeping both hands on the gunwales. Stay low as you move about. In tandem canoes, one paddler should steady the canoe while the other paddler climbs in. Then, the first aboard should steady the canoe for the other paddler. In swift water, the paddler down current enters first and exits last; this makes it easier for the up-current paddler, while on land, to hold the canoe and keep it from swinging out into the stream short one paddler.

Many whitewater kayakers "seal launch," that is, they climb in on shore and push themselves and their boats into the water. This is not recommended, because it can damage the kayak as well as the fragile margins of rivers.

Coaming is the raised edging around the cockpit for keeping water out.

The J-stroke is an advanced stroke that takes a lot of practice.

Before you enter a kayak, put on your spray skirt. To steady yourself as you slip into your craft, place your paddle shaft against the *coaming* at the back of your boat's cockpit so that one blade is touching ground. Grasp the center of the paddle shaft and the cockpit coaming with one hand and ease yourself into the boat. Attach the spray skirt to the cockpit rim and you're ready to paddle off. Reverse this process to climb out.

Paddling Forward in a Straight Line

In a solo canoe, the J-stroke allows for a smooth, continuous forward stroke that keeps the boat on course with minimum effort. Apply only as much "J" to the stroke as is needed to keep the canoe going straight. Too much will turn the canoe. If necessary, review and practice the J-stroke solo in flatwater by picking a distant target and paddling to it in a straight line. In a tandem canoe, the bow paddler should do a forward stroke while the stern paddler does a J-stroke to keep the boat on course.

In a kayak, forward motion is achieved with the basic forward stroke. Stroke first on one side and then on the other. Review and practice the forward stroke on flatwater if necessary.

Backpaddling

Canoeists and kayakers use backstrokes to backpaddle, that is, to slow or reverse the forward motion of the boat. You may need to backpaddle to

- Run a set of waves slowly, giving your boat's bow a chance to rise above a wave so that it will stay dry.

- Give yourself more time to turn or move your boat sideways.

- Keep control in swift water, allowing more time to move left or right or to stop.

- Slow your boat in anticipation of shallow water, rocks, or sleepers.

- Stop your boat so you can scout or take a break.

- Back ferry (or "set") is to move your craft left or right in the current while still facing downstream.

Sideslips are very useful on shallow rivers. Practice them in quiet water by paddling forward and then executing a stationary draw *or* pry (solo) or draw *and* pry (tandem).

Sideslips

Sideslipping on a river means moving your boat to one side or another far enough to miss a rock or other obstacle and then continue paddling on downstream. Draws and pries are the two strokes you will need to do a good sideslip.

Suppose you are moving faster than the current going downstream. A rock becomes visible directly downstream and you want to dodge it on its river left. If you are in a solo canoe or kayak, execute a draw or pry until your heading is clear of the rock. Once your path is clear of the rock, continue paddling downstream.

In a tandem canoe, one paddler draws and the other pries. The boat will move away from a pry and toward a draw stroke. The paddler in the stern should take his cues from the bow paddler, who has a much better view of the obstacles and hazards ahead. As the bow paddler communicates —either by his strokes or verbally—the need to avoid an object, the stern paddler should perform a matching draw or pry stroke to move the boat sideways.

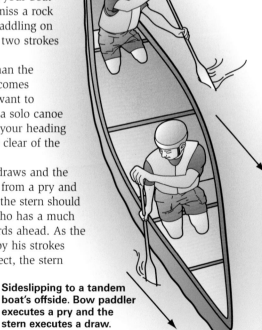

Sideslipping to a tandem boat's offside. Bow paddler executes a pry and the stern executes a draw.

Eddy Turns

Tandem canoes dance from eddy to eddy by virtue of technique and communication. Bow and stern paddlers must talk to each other about where they are going and how they are going to get there. Pause at the top of a rapid and have a chat about how you want to run the rapid.

As you paddle downstream, you will want to stop in an eddy to rest or to scout a rapid below. The maneuver to enter an eddy while heading downstream is called an eddy turn. Later you will learn how to exit an eddy using a peel out. When you have learned how to move in and out of eddies with confidence and ease, you will have passed a major whitewater skills milestone.

Entering an eddy while moving downstream in a boat can be challenging, especially if the current is fast. Here are the basic steps to doing an eddy turn.

Step 1—Start well upstream and begin angling your boat so that when it reaches the top of the eddy, the boat will cross the eddy line at about a 45-degree angle.

Step 2—Aim the bow so it crosses the eddy line as close as possible to the top of the eddy. Avoid hitting the obstacle that is creating the eddy.

Step 3—As soon as possible after the bow crosses the eddy line, plant the paddle in the upstream current of the eddy so that the rest of the boat will swing around the paddle as the pivot point.

Step 4—Just before and as the boat enters the eddy, the paddler or paddlers must tilt the boat (not themselves) into the turn by using the lower body and shifting more weight onto one knee in a canoe or one hip in a kayak. The upper body moves very little.

The strokes used by whitewater paddlers to do an eddy turn depend on whether the maneuver is done solo or in tandem and whether it is done in the onside or offside position. Technically, kayakers do not have an onside or offside since they have a paddle blade on each side of the boat. For the purposes of this section, the kayaker's onside position will refer to the side of the body with the dominant arm and will correspond to the onside position for solo canoeists.

For kayakers and solo canoeists, an onside eddy turn uses the forward stroke to build up enough momentum for the boat to cross the eddy line at a 45-degree angle. As the bow and then the paddler's body enter the eddy, a Duffek stroke is performed

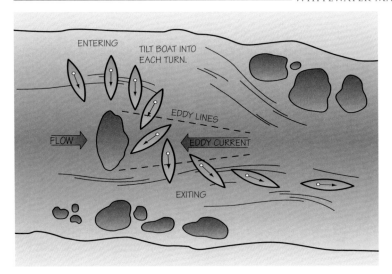

Eddy turn—entering and exiting an eddy

followed by a Duffek maneuver (a draw to the bow and then a forward stroke). For tandem canoeists, the bow paddler does a Duffek after his body has crossed the eddy line while the stern paddler does a quick draw stroke followed by a series of forward sweeps. Once the stern has entered the eddy, the bow paddler does the Duffek maneuver and the stern paddler does a forward stroke to move up to the head of the eddy.

An offside eddy turn is more difficult than an onside turn. For kayakers, the offside turn is performed like the onside turn except with the other blade. Solo canoeists perform the same steps as for the onside turn, but they must use a cross Duffek followed by a cross Duffek maneuver (cross draw to the bow and then a cross forward).

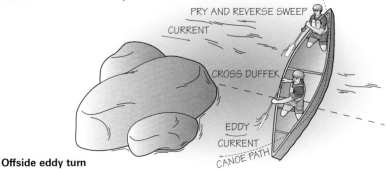

Offside eddy turn

Tandem paddlers in a canoe use the same approach to the eddy—including the angle and lean of the boat—as for the onside eddy turn. However, instead of a Duffek, the bow paddler does a cross Duffek. The stern paddler does a quick pry before the boat crosses the eddy line, followed if necessary by a small reverse sweep or quick pry off the stern gunwale, sometimes combined with a low brace. When the stern has entered the eddy, the bow paddler does a cross Duffek maneuver, which is a stationary cross-bow draw followed by a cross-bow forward stroke. Once in the eddy, the stern paddler performs a forward stroke or J-stroke.

Kayakers and solo canoeists accomplish eddy turns using a variety of strokes. A forward stroke, usually a J-stroke, combined with a forward sweep, draw or cross-bow draw, should push you in and then turn you in an eddy. Take one more stroke than you think you need to cross that eddy line. A Duffek stroke often will work well. As in tandem canoeing, a solo boat should enter the eddy at right angles, tilt into the turn, and have the right amount of speed to complete the maneuver.

Peel Outs

The peel out maneuver is used to exit an eddy and reenter the main current of the river. Peel outs are easier than eddy turns since you don't have to worry about maneuvering in a fast-moving downstream current. On the other hand, you will not have the speed that comes from the current because you have to cross the eddy line to exit. When done correctly with the right combination of speed, angle, and lean, any paddler can do a smart-looking turn into the current without a set of complicated strokes.

Here are the basic steps to safely doing a peel out:

Step 1—Exiting the eddy requires the boat to have sufficient speed to clear the eddy line. Position the boat near the eddy line and toward the bottom of the eddy so that you can take several strokes before exiting.

Step 2—Exit at the top of the eddy as close as possible to the start of the eddy line at about a 45-degree angle. Keep in mind: The faster the downstream current, the smaller the angle of entry.

Step 3—As the bow crosses the eddy line, tilt the boat downstream by shifting more weight onto one knee in a canoe or one hip in a kayak. Your upper body should move only slightly.

To do an onside peel out for kayakers and solo canoeists, paddle forward with enough speed to clear the eddy. Solo canoeists may need to use a combination of the cross forward stroke, forward stroke, and J-stroke to exit the eddy at the correct angle. As the bow begins to cross the eddy line, shift your weight to the downstream side of the boat. Keep paddling forward to maintain your momentum. Only *after* your body has crossed the eddy line should you do a turning stroke such as a bow draw, stern pry, Duffek, or Duffek maneuver. In many instances—if you have the right momentum and lean—the current will turn your bow downstream without any turning stroke at all.

Tandem canoeists doing an onside peel out follow the same steps as solo canoeists, but have the advantage of two paddlers to build up speed to exit the eddy. Once across the eddy line, the bow paddler does a turning stroke such as a Duffek while the stern paddler continues to power the boat out of the eddy with forward or J-strokes. As the bow of the boat begins to turn downstream, the stern paddler can do forward sweeps if there is enough speed and momentum to carry the boat out of the eddy.

With two paddlers in the boat, it is important to coordinate the downstream lean so both are leaning the boat in the same direction at the same time.

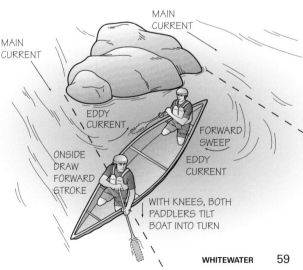

In the peel out, note how both paddlers use their left knees to lean into and tilt the boat into the turn.

MAIN CURRENT

MAIN CURRENT

MAIN CURRENT

EDDY CURRENT

FORWARD SWEEP

EDDY CURRENT

ONSIDE DRAW FORWARD STROKE

WITH KNEES, BOTH PADDLERS TILT BOAT INTO TURN

An offside peel out incorporates all the same features of the onside peel out except that the turning strokes are different. For kayakers, the opposite paddle blade is used for the turning stroke. After crossing the eddy line, solo canoeists can use a variety of turning strokes, including a forward sweep, cross bow draw, cross Duffek, or cross Duffek maneuver. Tandem canoeists use a combination of a cross Duffek or cross Duffek maneuver in the bow while the stern paddler does a low bracing reverse sweep or simply powers ahead with a forward or J-stroke.

Ferrying Upstream and Downstream

Upstream (forward) ferries and downstream (back) ferries move you sideways across the current. In an upstream ferry, you face upstream and paddle forward with your bow at an angle to the current. You move across the current in the direction your bow is pointing. To perform a downstream ferry, you face downstream and backpaddle with your stern pointed upstream at an angle to the current. You move across the current in the direction your stern is facing.

To perform a successful upstream ferry, begin by turning your boat until it faces upstream. As you start paddling, adjust the ferry angle—the angle of the boat compared to the upstream—to about 10 degrees. If you are moving out of an eddy into the current, enter the current as if you were doing a peel out by exiting the eddy at about a 45-degree angle and leaning downstream. Instead of turning downstream, paddle directly into the upstream current as quickly as possible.

Kayakers and solo canoeists use the forward stroke with an occasional stern draw or pry stroke to keep them angled into the current. In a tandem canoe, the bow paddler does forward strokes while the stern paddler does combinations of strokes to keep the boat at the desired angle to the current.

Gradually increase the ferry angle by allowing the bow of your boat to point a little to one side of where the current is flowing. Use a small ferry angle if the current is fast and a larger angle if the current is slow. The smaller the ferry angle, the less your boat will drift downstream, but your crossing

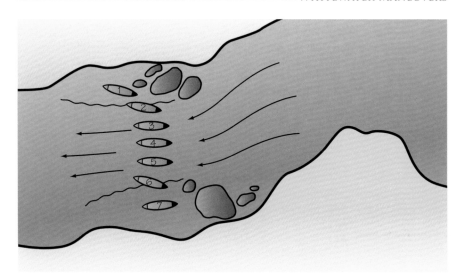

Upstream ferry across river to avoid obstacles.

speed will be slower. On the other hand, if you use a large
ferry angle, you will get across the river faster, but you will
end up farther downstream. Your paddling counters the river's
tendency to pull you downstream, and your boat's angle off
the current allows the river to nudge you toward the far bank.
This can be tricky, so practice by ferrying across an easy
current with the goal of reducing the number of strokes
needed to cross the stream.

Downstream ferries are more difficult than upstream ferries.
To perform a successful downstream ferry, point the stern of
your boat almost directly upstream and exit into the current.
Kayakers and canoeists use backstrokes and control their angle
to the current with draws and pries. Tandem canoe paddlers
use the backstroke while doing a downstream ferry. The stern
paddler, with occasional help from the bow paddler, is responsible for steering the boat.

To keep the boat
at the correct
angle during a
downstream ferry,
the bow paddler
can steer by using
a combination
of backstrokes
with bow draws
and prys.

Remember: It is the angle of your boat to the current,
not to the shore, that determines your ferry angle.
Over time you will become skillful in reading currents
and upstream and downstream ferries will become
second nature.

River Signals

Running rapids takes teamwork. Teammates should discuss their run on an ongoing basis and make adjustments to any plan as needed. Sometimes, however, talk is impossible. Even a small riffle can muffle words, and roaring rapids often drown out speech altogether. For emergencies or times when talk is difficult, river runners make use of whistles and paddle signals to communicate. Review river signals before the beginning of every trip.

Here are important emergency and directional signals.

- **"Stop!"**
  Raise and lower a paddle horizontally over your head or hold both arms out at right angles to your body and wave them up and down.

- **"Help!"**
  Give three long blasts of your whistle. Or wave your paddle, your helmet, or PFD back and forth over your head.

- **"Are you OK?"**
  Raise one arm over your head, bend your elbow outward, and tap your helmet with your fingertips. To respond that you are OK to someone signaling you, return the same signal.

- **"Run down the center" or "Come ahead" or "All clear"** Hold your paddle blade in a vertical position above your head with the blade flat for maximum visibility.

- **"Run left"** As the lead paddler who has run the drop, you are facing back upstream and directing those following to run river left. Point your paddle in the direction you want others to follow, at a 45 degree angle, with the blade flat (for better visibility).

- **"Run right"** As the lead paddler who has run the drop, you are facing back upstream and directing those following to run river right. Point your paddle in the direction you want others to follow, at a 45 degree angle, with the blade flat (for better visibility).

Important: Always use directional paddle signals to indicate where the safe route through a drop lies. *Never point toward hazards.*

Portaging

Portaging is a normal part of running rivers. When you have scouted a stretch of river and determined that the rapids are impassable or beyond your capabilities or your equipment, it is time to portage (or carry) your canoe or kayak over land to a safer place on the river. Always portage around low-head dams and weirs or any sheer drop or strainer that cannot safely be avoided. Shallows may also require a portage. When assessing a rough stretch of river, a good rule is, "When in doubt, walk around."

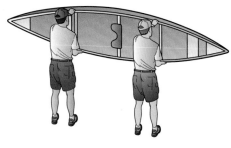

To portage a canoe with a yoke, position yourself near the bow of the canoe and your buddy near the stern. Reach across the canoe and grasp the gunwales, then in unison lift the canoe and flip it over your heads, turning yourselves forward as you do. As your partner stabilizes the canoe, walk your hands backward along the gunwales until you can tuck your shoulders against the yoke. Your partner is free to duck out from under the canoe, and you are ready to begin a portage. Your partner leads the way as you walk, alerting you to obstacles or turns.

With practice, one canoeist can lift a canoe for portaging. To begin, stand at one side of the upright canoe, near the stern and facing the bow. Grasp the gunwales, one in each hand, a few feet from the stern. Turn the canoe over and lift it over your head, allowing the bow to remain on the ground. Holding the gunwales, begin "walking" toward the bow. As you reach the center of the canoe, its weight will balance over your shoulders and the bow will lift off the ground. Ease the yoke onto your shoulders to carry the canoe.

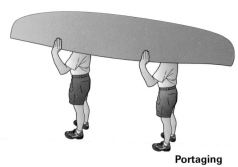

Portaging

If there is no portage yoke, the canoe can be transported using a two-man carry.

Many kayaks have toggles installed at the bow and stern, positioned for two people to lift and carry a craft. For a solo carry, reach across the cockpit, lift the kayak, and flip it onto your shoulder. (If the kayak is heavy, allow the stern to stay on the ground as you lift and position it.) Shift the cockpit on your shoulder to reach the kayak's balance point, and you should be ready for a relatively easy tote to your destination.

There's an old saying that no one ever drowned on a portage.

Carrying a kayak

Rescue Techniques

Every kayaker and canoeist capsizes from time to time. When-ever you take a spill, make the safety of the people involved your top priority. Equipment and gear can be replaced, people cannot. Practice to become adept at recovering from a capsize and learn to use a throw rope to rescue other paddlers.

Self-Rescue

When you capsize, follow these steps:

Step 1—If you can, stay in your righted boat, even if it is flooded. The hull can protect you from banging into obstacles. You may be able to climb back in (assisted or unassisted by other boats) and then paddle to shore. If you are in a kayak with or without a spray skirt or in a solo whitewater canoe with thigh straps, exit the boat as quickly as possible. You may have to pop the skirt or loosen the straps to free yourself from the boat. As you become more experienced, you can learn to right yourself using an Eskimo roll. Intermediate kayakers and advanced canoeists learn how to do the Eskimo roll so that if they turn over while in their boats, they can flip back up again without having to do a wet exit.

Step 2—If you have been tossed into the water, hold on to your boat. It will stay afloat, and it will be easy for rescuers to spot. Stay upstream of your boat so you do not get caught between your fast-moving boat and a hard obstacle like a boulder.

Step 3—In the following situations, swim aggressively for shore.

　　a. You have been thrown clear of your boat.

　　b. The water is very cold.

　　c. You are approaching worsening rapids.

　　d. No rescue is forthcoming.

Step 4—If you must ride out a rapid before swimming to safety or catching a rescue line, stay on your back in fast water, keeping your feet and legs floating high and downstream so they can act as shock absorbers to fend off rocks. Use a backstroke to maneuver past obstacles and keep an eye out for an eddy that might offer protection.

Step 5—Do not stand up in swift-moving water above your knees. If your feet were to become entrapped under rocks, the current could knock you over—either backward or forward—and then force your head under the water.

Step 6—If you find yourself being swept toward a strainer, change from a feetfirst position to an active headfirst swimming position with your head out of the water. Try to climb up on top of the strainer as far as you can get, and aggressively pull yourself onto it to avoid getting sucked underneath.

Step 7—When rescuers are trying to assist you, do all you can to help them help you.

Capsize Drills

Intentionally capsize your craft in calm water and practice recovering from the spills until your reactions become automatic.

To safely capsize a canoe, sit next to your paddling partner in the bottom of the canoe facing the same side. Let your legs hang over the gunwale. Put your hand nearest your partner on the gunwale behind you. Put your other hand on the gunwale in front of you. Rock forward and backward until the gunwale in front of you goes below the water level and the canoe begins to fill with water.

To practice a "wet exit" from a kayak, lean your body out over the water to cause your boat to capsize. Release the spray skirt from the coaming then lean forward with your forehead near the deck and push on the sides of the coaming with your hands. This will push you out of the kayak. When your legs and feet are clear, let them drop toward the bottom. Keep your grip on the coaming throughout the maneuver. When you are in the feet-down position in the water, bring your head up on one side of the capsized kayak. After completing the wet exit, turn the kayak so you can grab an end loop. Push or pull the kayak to shallow water, keeping it upside down so that the air trapped in the cockpit will keep the boat afloat.

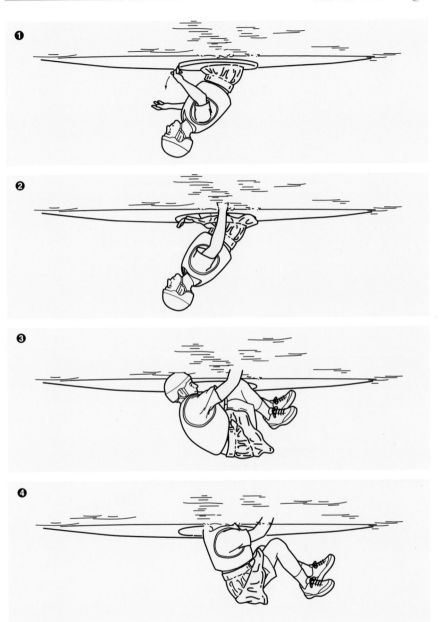

Capsize drill

Using a Throw Rope to Rescue Others

As you will recall, a throw rope is a floating rope that is stored in a throw bag. The rope will pay out neatly when the bag is tossed. A throw bag or a neatly coiled throw rope should always be secured in your craft so that it will be handy in a rescue situation, but not an entrapment hazard.

To rescue swimmers with a throw rope follow these steps:

Step 1—Remove enough rope from the bag so that you can throw the bag while holding on to the loose end of the rope with your other hand. Allow the remainder of the rope to stay in the bag. It will pay out when the bag is thrown. Be sure that the mouth of the bag is only halfway open.

Step 2—Get the attention of the person in the water by yelling, "Rope!" or giving a single blast of your whistle. Establish eye contact with the swimmer.

Step 3—Grasp or step on the free end of the rope and toss the bag at the swimmer. Aim at, or slightly beyond, the swimmer's head. If you miss, quickly restuff the bag or make arm-length coils of rope and try again.

Step 4—The victim should grab the rope and roll over on his back with the rope held in the middle of the chest and the rope going over the shoulder. The victim must not wrap the rope around a hand, or fasten the body in any way to the rope— just hold on. Either pull in the line to bring the person to safety, or allow the person to swing on the line to the bank. Walking your end of the line along the shore may help the swimmer cope with the current and avoid obstacles. Take great care not to be pulled into the water yourself. If necessary, sit down to help hold against the force on the line or belay the line around a tree or rock. Do not tie the rope to anything, which will help prevent the victim from being held under-water should he become entangled in the rope.

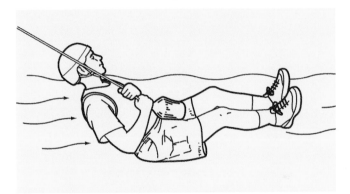

Practice Using the Throw Rope

Using a throw rope effectively takes practice. If you cannot practice in a controlled setting in a river, practice on land with a buddy by doing the following exercises.

1. Have your buddy pretend to be a slow-moving victim about 30 to 45 feet away. Toss the throw bag to him as he moves slowly by you.

2. Practice what you would do if you missed the throw the first time. Retrieve the rope by making long coils. Divide the coils between your hands and throw the rope again to your buddy. Practice both short and long throws and at different speeds as your buddy pretends to be in slow and fast moving currents.

Trip Planning

Before you head out to demonstrate your whitewater skills, work with your merit badge counselor or another qualified adult to select the river course and choose group participants. Consult with your counselor to make sure that the course is within the capabilities of all participants and that the equipment you will be using is appropriate for the activity.

Research and prepare a float plan that specifies your route. Be sure to include put in and take out points. Set up a schedule in which you determine how much time you will need to safely float the stretch of river you selected. Double check your equipment and review safety precautions and emergency procedures. Identify your options in the event of a problem with equipment, a sudden change in weather, or a medical emergency. A review of the BSA Safety Afloat principles and the American Whitewater safety guidelines will help you with these tasks.

Obtaining Necessary Permissions

The use of many rivers is governed by special rules and permits. Stay on the right side of the law, and get permission to float before you go. You will often find that a state or federal agency holds jurisdiction over the stretch of river you want to run. If you will be crossing private property, always get permission from the landowner. Local boating shops, river guidebooks, maps, and government-agency Web sites can provide information about whom you need to contact.

Personal and Group Equipment

Before you head out on the river, always double-check that you have both personal and group essentials necessary for a safe whitewater outing. This checklist provides some guidelines, but you may need to adapt it to reflect your specific needs and the purpose of your trip.

Personal Essentials

- [ ] PFD with whistle
- [ ] Helmet
- [ ] Pocketknife
- [ ] Spare clothing
- [ ] Rain gear
- [ ] Unbreakable water bottles filled with water
- [ ] Lunch and/or snacks
- [ ] Sun protection (including sunscreen, brimmed hat, and sunglasses with a strap)
- [ ] Map and compass
- [ ] Spare glasses (if you wear them)
- [ ] First-aid kit

Place everything that must stay dry in waterproof containers such as dry bags, boxes, buckets, or barrels. Items that need to stay dry include food, spare clothing, first-aid kits, maps, sleeping bags, tents, and other camping equipment.

Use cam straps, bungee cords, and pieces of rope to secure items and equipment so they will not fall out past the gunwales if you capsize. Dry bags are often lashed in gunwale to gunwale. All loose rope should be stowed out of the way. It is vital that your lashing does not pose an entrapment hazard.

Packing for a whitewater trip

Essential Group Equipment

Group equipment should be evenly distributed among all the boats. Here is a general list of equipment. Adjust your own list to suit the length of time you will be out and the number of people participating.

- ☐ Spare paddle (at least one per party, preferably one per boat)

- ☐ Flotation (air bags or foam) in each boat to keep the boat afloat if you capsize

- ☐ For canoes: A bailer made of a cut-out gallon plastic jug, attached to the floor of your boat with a very short length of line or webbing and a plastic fastener

- ☐ Large absorbent sponge to soak up splashes and clean up sand and mud

- ☐ For open canoes: Bow and stern lines (painters) securely attached. Use ropes at least 5 feet longer than your boat, $\frac{5}{16}$ inch or $\frac{3}{8}$ inch in diameter. Secure them to the canoe so that they are readily available but will not entangle feet and legs in case of a spill.

- ☐ Water filter or water treatment tablets. During a whitewater outing, you'll need as much water as you would during a strenuous hike. Having a means of treating water while afloat will help avoid dehydration.

- ☐ Throw rope in a bag
- ☐ First-aid kit
- ☐ Waterproof matches, lighter, candle, or fire starter
- ☐ Duct tape and a repair kit
- ☐ Handheld bilge pump (optional)
- ☐ Camping equipment (for overnight trips)

River Etiquette

River etiquette is simply showing courtesy and respect for people you encounter on the river including other boaters, fishers, and swimmers. Here are some common guidelines for being a good ambassador for whitewater paddling.

- Yield the right of way to crafts with less maneuverability such as rafts and boats running straight through a rapid.

- When running down a river, try to pick a path that will not interfere with another paddler playing in a hole or surfing a wave.

- Do not tailgate through a rapid. Leave plenty of space between boats.

- If an eddy is already full of boats, wait upstream until there is room or find another one downstream.

- Pass other boats with care. Do not try to pass in a rapid.

- Allow faster boats to pass.

- Stay out of other boaters' way. Pass fishers quietly and give them as much space as possible.

- Share play spots with other boaters and wait your turn.

- Do not crowd boating classes or novice boaters.

Bear in mind that river recreation often concentrates a lot of traffic into a narrow corridor. Many of our rivers are in danger of being loved to death. Take care of stream banks when you launch and land your boat, and walk gently on the land. Practice Leave No Trace principles. Respect the river so that future generations will be able to enjoy the thrill, mystery, and beauty of whitewater paddling.

Whitewater Resources

Scouting Literature

Boy Scout Handbook; Fieldbook; Deck of First Aid; Emergency First Aid pocket guide; *Be Prepared First Aid Book;* Kayaking BSA Award application; *Canoeing, Rowing,* and *Small-Boat Sailing* merit badge pamphlets

Visit the Boy Scouts of America's official retail Web site (with your parent's permission) at *http:// www.scoutstuff.org* for a complete listing of all merit badge pamphlets and other helpful Scouting materials and supplies.

Books

Bennett, Jeff. *The Complete Whitewater Rafter.* International Marine/Ragged Mountain Press, 1996.

———. *The Essential Whitewater Kayaker.* International Marine/ Ragged Mountain Press, 1999.

Blaine, Mark. *Whitewater: The Thrill and Skill of Running the World's Great Rivers.* Black Dog and Leventhal Publishers, 2001.

Bechdel, Les. *River Rescue: A Manual for Whitewater Safety.* Appalachian Mountain Club Books, 1997.

Grant, Gordon. *Trailside Guide: Canoeing.* W. W. Norton & Company, 2003.

Harrison, Dave. *Canoeing: The Complete Guide to Equipment and Technique.* Stackpole Books, 1996.

Jackson, Eric. *Whitewater Paddling: Strokes & Concepts.* Stackpole Books, 1999.

Krauzer, Steven M. *Trailside Guide: Kayaking.* W. W. Norton & Company, 2003.

Mason, Bill. *Path of the Paddle: An Illustrated Guide to the Art of Canoeing* (revised and updated by Paul Mason). Firefly Books, 1999.

Mason, Paul. *Thrill of the Paddle: The Art of Whitewater Canoeing.* Firefly Books, 1999.

Nealy, William. *Kayak: A Manual of Technique.* Menasha Ridge Press, 1986.

Ray, Slim. *The Canoe Handbook: Techniques for Mastering the Sport of Canoeing.* Stackpole Books, 1992.

World Class Readings 1

High Beginning
A Reading Skills Text

Bruce Rogers

McGraw-Hill

World Class Readings 1, 1st Edition

Published by McGraw-Hill ESL/ELT, a business unit of The McGraw-Hill Companies, Inc.,
1221 Avenue of the Americas, New York, NY 10020. Copyright © 2005 by The McGraw-Hill
Companies, Inc. All rights reserved. No part of this publication may be reproduced or distributed
in any form or by any means, or stored in a database or retrieval system, without the prior written
consent of The McGraw-Hill Companies, Inc., including, but not limited to, in any network or
other electronic storage or transmission, or broadcast for distance learning.

ISBN: 0-07-282545-6

  6 7 8 9 IBT/IBT 09

ISBN: 0-07-111008-9

1 2 3 4 5 6 7 8 9 VLP 09 08 07 06 05 04

Photo Credits
Page 1, Hulton Archive/Getty Images. Page 5, Douglas McFadd/Getty Images. Page 13, (c) Murdo Macleod/Corbis
Sygma. Page 17, Courtesy of Warner Bros./Getty Images. Page 25, Hulton Archive/Getty Images. Page 30, Hulton
Archive/Getty Images. Page 33, Vanni/Art Resource, NY. Page 38, Nina Leen/Time Life Pictures/Getty Images. Page
42, The Picture Desk/The Art Archive. Page 43, Setboun/ Corbis. Page 45, Anthony Verde/Time Life Pictures/Getty
Images. Page 45, Hans Reinhard/Photo Researchers Inc. Page 50, Art Wolfe/Photo Researchers, Inc. Page 54, A. N.
T./Photo Researchers, Inc. Page 55, Steve Kaufman/CORBIS. Page 61, Gregory Ochocki/Photo Researchers, Inc.
Page 73, Darren McNamara/Allsport/Getty Images. Page 78, Paul Buck/AFP/Corbis. Page 84, Esperanto League for
North America, ELNA. Page 95, The Granger Collection. Page 99, The Granger Collection. Page 100, Mallory and
Irvine Expedition/Jim Fagiolo/Getty Images. Page 109, Roger Harris/Photo Researchers, Inc. Page 114, Getty
Images. Page 116, Hulton Archive/Getty Images. Page 122, Jim Erickson/CORBIS. Page 125, Bettmann/CORBIS.
Page 132, Wang Jeng-Jyi. Page 135, Wang Jeng-Jyi. Page 143, Jack Dabaghian/Reuters NewMedia Inc./CORBIS.
Page 147, Jack Dabaghian/Reuters NewMedia Inc./CORBIS. Page 155, A. Gragera, Latin Stock/Science Photo
Library. Page 158, Hulton Archive/Getty Images. Page 159, Hulton Archive/Getty Images.

Editorial director: *Tina B. Carver*
Senior sponsoring editor: *Thomas Healy*
Developmental editor: *Susan Johnson*
Editorial assistant: *Kasey Williamson*
Illustrations: *Hal Just*
Interior design and cover design: *A Good Thing, Inc.*
Production: *Carol Sailors, A Good Thing, Inc.*

Contents

Introduction

World Class Readings 1 is a high beginning level text for nonnative speakers of English. It is part of the *World Class Readings* series. The primary focus of this series is reading, but there are also exercises to improve students' skills in listening, speaking, and writing. The readings are appropriate both for students learning English for strictly academic purposes and for those learning English for more general reasons.

World Class Readings practices and develops many of the skills that are needed to do well on standardized English tests, such as the TOEFL®, TOEIC®, and IELTS®. Using this series, therefore, is a good way for a student to prepare for those important exams.

Organization of the Book

World Class Readings 1 consists of fourteen units centered around a reading. Each unit has the following components:

1. Warm-Up Questions

This section serves to draw students into the reading in a number of ways. The questions prompt students to skim the text and use the pictures that open the unit to make predictions about the reading. They encourage students to share information they may already have about the topic and solicit students' opinions on issues that are raised in the reading.

2. Vocabulary Preview

This section consists of short segments taken directly from the reading. A word or a phrase in each segment is highlighted . These items are vocabulary terms that are important to an overall understanding of the reading.

3. While You Read

This exercise supplies a list of important topics that are discussed in the reading, presented out of order. Students need to number these topics in the order in which they appear in the reading. The exercise helps students understand the structure of the reading and provides practice in skimming for important points.

4. The Reading

The reading, ranging in length from about 400 to 600 words, is the heart of each unit. Cultural and topic-specific vocabulary and concepts that might be unfamiliar to readers are footnoted.

5. Understanding the Reading

This section, consisting of eight multiple-choice questions, builds students' comprehension of the reading. Most of these are explicit detail questions that can be answered by skimming the reading, but some require students to draw inferences from the reading. This part of the unit is closest to the reading section of a number of standardized exams, including the TOEFL® and TOEIC®.

6. Vocabulary Building

This exercise consists of vocabulary taken from the reading and eight sentences unrelated to the reading. Each sentence has a blank that students fill in with a word from the vocabulary list. Students use the context of the sentence to make the choice.

7. Reading Skill

This part of the unit focuses on individual reading skills and features an exercise that allows students to apply that skill to the reading. A comprehensive list of these skills appears on pages 171-173.

8. Focus on Listening

The audio program for *World Class Readings* contains statements about the reading passages. Students listen to these statements and answer true or false questions about the reading. This activity provides listening practice and helps prepare students for certain listening activities in standardized tests.

9. Writing and Discussion Questions

This section consists of topics related to the theme of the reading. In most units, at least one of these items asks students who have Internet access to use the Web as a research tool and as a source of further reading material on the same theme.

10. Crossword Puzzle

Each unit ends with a crossword puzzle. The words used to solve the puzzle come from the Vocabulary Preview and Vocabulary Building exercises and from topic-specific vocabulary in the reading. It serves as a review of vocabulary introduced in the unit.

The Teacher's Manual

The *Teacher's Manual* contains quizzes, one for each unit, which can be photocopied and given to students as a graded test or as a final review of the unit. The *Teacher's Manual* also has a complete answer key, as well as an audio script for the listening activity.

I hope that the students and teachers who use this book will find it enjoyable. The English language skills and the information in the readings are meant to be fun, as well as useful. I hope that they provide glimpses into that huge, diverse, and interdependent culture, not of one country, but of the world.

Bruce Rogers

The author and the publisher would like to thank all the people whose comments, reviews, and assistance were invaluable in the development of *World Class Readings*.

The author would particularly like to thank Thomas Healy for his insight, his humor, and his many kindnesses. He is a world class editor.

It's the 21st Century. . . . Where's My Robot?

Fig 1.1 A domestic robot, developed by Quasar industries in America, vacuuming the house, November 1968

Before You Read

➤ Warm-Up Questions

Discuss these questions in pairs or groups. Share your ideas with the class.

1. Look at the photo and the title of the reading. What will this reading be about?

2. This reading is about robots that are designed to do housework. What is housework? Do you think robots will ever be able to do this kind of work?

➤ Vocabulary Preview

These statements come from the reading "It's the 21st Century. . . . Where's My Robot?" Read each statement and then answer the questions. Check your answers before you begin the reading.

The Jetsons had a housekeeper named Rosie.

1. What kind of work does a *housekeeper* do?

    (A) Cooking and cleaning
    (B) Protecting a house
    (C) Electrical work

Robots do various jobs today. They are often used in manufacturing . They paint and assemble cars and put together electronic devices .

2. *Manufacturing* means . . .

    (A) making art.
    (B) moving things.
    (C) making things in factories.

3. Circle the phrase that has the same meaning as *assemble*.

4. *Devices* are . . .

    (A) computer programs.
    (B) trucks and heavy vehicles.
    (C) small machines.

For example, they were used to explore Mars, to investigate the great pyramids in Egypt, and to search the wreckage of the World Trade Center in New York City.

5. Circle two other words close in meaning to *explore*.

SONY's robot dog Aibo is a popular toy. It never bites, barks , or makes messes.

6. When a dog *barks*, it . . .

    (A) makes a loud noise.
    (B) chases something, such as a cat.
    (C) sleeps for a short time.

There is a robot bartender that can make drinks and tell jokes .

7. To *tell jokes* is to . . .

   (A) give advice to customers.
   (B) say something funny.
   (C) clean glasses.

Some engineers believe that it is not practical to build all-purpose robots in the near future. They think each family will own several tiny robots, each designed to do one chore .

8. When something is not *practical,* it is not . . . to do.

   (A) easy
   (B) necessary
   (C) pleasant

9. A *chore* is a . . .

   (A) location.
   (B) task.
   (C) price.

There might be one robot to do the dusting , one to wash the windows, and one to clean the floors.

10. Which item is used to do *dusting* ?

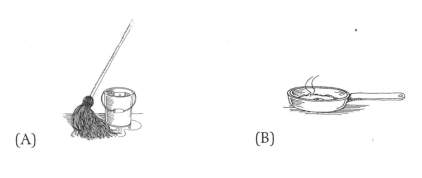

(A)   (B)

(C)

While You Read

Here are six points that are discussed in the reading. There is one point for each paragraph. While you read, put the points in order from 1 to 6.

_____ A Robot like Rosie: many years away
_____ Robots in factories and dangerous places
_____ The Jetsons' robot: not an accurate prediction of the future
_____ Single-purpose cleaning robots
_____ Entertainment robots
_____ Why household robots are not·popular today

IT'S THE 21ST CENTURY.... WHERE'S MY ROBOT?

1   Around forty years ago, there was a cartoon show[1] on television called The Jetsons. The Jetsons were a family of the future. George Jetson went to work in a rocket, and his wife Jane shopped for groceries on television. The Jetsons had a housekeeper named Rosie. Rosie washed dishes and vacuumed, but she wasn't an ordinary housekeeper. Rosie was a robot. At the time, some viewers thought the cartoon might predict the real future. In some ways it did. For example, some people shop on line.[2] But we don't have robots as housekeepers. At least, not yet.

2   Robots do various jobs today. They are often used in manufacturing. They paint and assemble cars and put together electronic devices. Also, robots are used for jobs that are difficult or dangerous for humans. For example, they were used to explore the planet Mars, to investigate the interior of the great pyramids in Egypt, and to search the wreckage of the World Trade Center in New York City.

Fig. 1.2 Vacuum cleaning robot.

3   Some robots in use today entertain people. SONY's robot dog Aibo is a popular toy. It never bites, barks, or makes messes. There are also robot cats and mice. Samsung Corporation has even made a robot goldfish. There is a robot bartender that can make drinks and tell jokes.

4   There ARE robots that can do housework. Several vacuum cleaning robots are available. However, not many people buy these products. Why not? The main reason is cost. These robots are expensive. Another reason is that robot cleaners don't always do a good job. A third reason is power. Most of these robots use batteries for power, and the batteries do not last long without recharging.

5   Some engineers believe that it is not practical to build all-purpose robots in the near future. They think each family will own several tiny robots, each designed to do one chore. There might be one robot to do the dusting, one to wash the windows, and one to clean the floors.

6   Today, like the Jetsons, we are living in the "future," but few of us have robots in our houses. Unfortunately, a humanlike robot like Rosie that can cook gourmet meals, walk the dog, and change the baby's diapers is still many, many years away.

Notes

1. A *cartoon show* is a television program that features animated characters instead of live actors.

2. *On line* means using a computer and the Internet.

After You Read

➤ Understanding the Reading

Answer these multiple-choice questions to see how well you understood the reading.

1. What was Rosie's relationship to George Jetson?

   (A) She was his wife.
   (B) She was his daughter.
   (C) She was his housekeeper.

2. *The Jetsons* accurately predicted the way some people today . . .

   (A) go to work.
   (B) prepare their meals.
   (C) do their shopping.

3. Aibo is a robot . . .

   (A) dog.
   (B) cat.
   (C) goldfish.

4. Paragraph 2 gives examples of robots used in dangerous jobs. Which of these is also a good example of that?

   (A) Robots waiting on tables at a restaurant
   (B) Robots washing the windows of a tall building
   (C) Robots cleaning swimming pools

5. What is the main reason people do NOT buy a household robot today?

   (A) They are not safe.
   (B) They are too expensive.
   (C) They are too hard to use.

6. What problem do people have with the batteries in household robots?

(A) They must be recharged often.
(B) They are too heavy.
(C) They are not attractive.

7. What do the engineers in paragraph 5 predict?

(A) All families will soon own an all-purpose robot.
(B) Robots will never be able to do housework.
(C) There may be many small robots to do specific jobs.

8. When does the author think there will be a robot like Rosie?

(A) In a few months
(B) In a few years
(C) Many years in the future

➤ Vocabulary Building

Fill in the blanks in the sentences below with one of these words from the reading.

recharge   interior   viewers   gourmet
predict   housekeeper   all-purpose   assemble

1. A: Are you and your girlfriend going to a _____ restaurant for your birthday?

   B: No, we're going to a pizza place. I like pizza better than fancy food.

2. Some people use crystal balls and others use playing cards to try to _____ the future.

3. My cell phone doesn't work. I forgot to _____ the battery.

4. This paint is for the _____ of the house, not for the outside.

5. I wish we had a _____ to clean up our apartment.

6. A: I bought this toy for my nephew, but it is really difficult to

   _____.

   B: I'm sure you could put it together if you read the directions.

7. More _____ watch television on Sunday night than on any other night.

8. This _____ cleaning product should clean everything, but it doesn't clean anything!

Reading Skill: Identifying Main Ideas

A main idea is a key point in a reading—in a paragraph, a section of the reading, or the whole reading. Main ideas are stated in "summary" sentences. For example, a *topic sentence* sums up the main idea of a paragraph. A *thesis statement* sums up the main idea of a reading.

Where do you find summary sentences? These sentences often come at the beginning or end of a reading or paragraph. However, location varies. And in some cases, the main idea is not stated directly at all.

Recognizing main ideas takes practice. Following are some ways to identify a sentence that states a main idea.

- Main idea sentences are not too specific. They do not talk about only one idea or a detail. In other words, the main idea is not too "small" for the information it covers.

- Main idea sentences are not too general. They do not talk about ideas or details outside of the passage. In other words, they are not too "large" for the information they cover.

- The main idea sentence sums up the passage exactly. No more and no less. In other words, it explains all of the information in the passage.

Look at this paragraph:

One way to design better robots is to learn from animals. Scientists study insects, snakes, lizards, and other creatures to see how they operate. Then they design robots that operate in similar ways. For example, a group of Australian scientists is studying the eyes of the fiddler crab. The fiddler crab has eyes that are primitive but work very well. The scientists hope to develop "eyes" for robots similar to the eyes of these crabs.

What is the main idea?

(A) Scientists in Australia are studying the eyes of fiddler crabs.
(B) Scientists are learning how to develop better robots.
(C) Scientists study animals to design better robots.

The statement that best summarizes the passage is C. Choice A focuses on one animal that scientists study. It is only an example, and it is too specific. Choice B is too general. The passage is about studying animals when designing robots, not about designing better robots in general.

Exercise: Identify the main ideas of the reading. Put a checkmark (✓) if the statement states a main idea. Put a **G** if it is too general. Put an **S** if it is too specific.

Paragraph 1

_____ (A) Many predictions about the future do not come true.

_____ (B) Household robots such as the one in *The Jetsons* are still not available.

_____ (C) George Jetson went to work in a rocket.

Paragraph 2

_____ (A) Robots are used today in factories and dangerous situations.

_____ (B) Robots have been successful in most fields of activity.

_____ (C) Robots have been used to explore the planet Mars.

Paragraph 3

_____ (A) The entertainment industry is a very important one.

_____ (B) The robot bartender makes drinks and tells jokes.

_____ (C) Entertainment is another field in which robots are successful.

Paragraph 4

_____ (A) Robots do not always do a good job.

_____ (B) The batteries on robot housecleaners don't last very long.

_____ (C) Although housecleaning robots have been built, they are not very popular with customers.

Paragraph 5

_____ (A) Rather than using one all-purpose robot, people might use a number of small, single-purpose robots.

_____ (B) One small robot could dust the house.

_____ (C) Some engineers believe it is better to design products with one use rather than products that have many functions.

Paragraph 6

_____ (A) It will be many years before robots can cook gourmet meals.

_____ (B) A good all-purpose robot will not be available in the near future.

_____ (C) Cartoons are not good predictors of the future.

The Whole Reading

_____ (A) Robots are useful tools today, and they will be even more useful in the future.

_____ (B) Entertainment robots and industrial robots are in common use today.

_____ (C) Although robots have been successful in some fields, household robots are still not in general use.

➤ Focus on Listening

Listen to the recording of the reading "It's the 21st Century. . . . Where's My Robot?" You will hear this reading two times. The first time, read along with the recording. Listen to the sound and tone of the words. The second time, listen for meaning. Do not look at the reading. Try to follow the ideas by listening only.

As you listen the second time, the speaker will stop occasionally and make statements about the reading. Decide if the statements are true or false. Fill in the space of the circled T or F according to what you hear and remember from the reading.

1. Ⓣ Ⓕ   5. Ⓣ Ⓕ

2. Ⓣ Ⓕ   6. Ⓣ Ⓕ

3. Ⓣ Ⓕ   7. Ⓣ Ⓕ

4. Ⓣ Ⓕ   8. Ⓣ Ⓕ

≫ Writing and Discussion Questions

Work with a partner or group to answer these questions.

1. Imagine that you can buy a robot which can do only one task. What kind of a robot would you buy? Explain.

2. Using the Internet, visit several sites that discuss robots. Try to find some basic information about two types of robots. Write several sentences about the robots that you choose. Try to find pictures of the robots. Share the information that you learn with the class.

3. One day, robots might take care of very old or sick people. What are other ways that robots can help people?

» Crossword Puzzle

Complete the puzzle with words from the reading.

Across

4 *The Jetsons* was an animated _____ show.

6 The Jetsons had a robot for a _____.

7 _____ Jetson was George's wife.

9 It will be a long time before robots can cook _____ dinners.

12 Robots are used to make electronic _____.

Down

1 George Jetson went to work in a _____.

2 Robots explored the _____ of a pyramid in Egypt.

3 Robots are used to paint and _____ automobiles.

5 The Jetsons' housekeeping robot was named _____.

8 _____ is the name of SONY's robot dog.

10 Robots were used to explore the planet _____.

11 Some engineers predict that families will own several _____ robots designed for specific chores.

J. K. Rowling: A Magical Author

Fig. 2.1 J. K. Rowling writing.

Before You Read

❯ Warm-Up Questions

Discuss these questions in pairs or groups. Share your ideas with the class.

1. This reading is about the author (writer) J. K. Rowling. Do you know what kind of books she writes?

2. Have you read any Harry Potter books or seen any Harry Potter movies? Why or why not?

⟫ Vocabulary Preview

These statements come from the reading "J. K. Rowling: A Magical Author."
Read each statement and then answer the questions. Check your answers before
you begin the reading.

When Rowling was nine, her family moved to a village called Tutshill. Her parents
wanted to live in a small town.

1. Find the phrase that is close in meaning to *village*. Circle that phrase.

However, her school was small and old-fashioned .

2. A school that is *old-fashioned* is . . .

   (A) small.
   (B) expensive.
   (C) not modern.

Rowling says that she was shy and was not good at sports.

3. A *shy* person . . .

   (A) is not completely honest.
   (B) is very creative.
   (C) does not like to talk to people.

On the trip, she had an idea about a boy who lives with a family that mistreats him.

4. A family that *mistreats* a child . . .

   (A) gives the child treats.
   (B) is not nice to the child.
   (C) teaches the child many things.

Although the boy doesn't realize it, he is a wizard !

5. A *wizard* is a . . .

   (A) magician.
   (B) genius.
   (B) spy.

After her divorce, Rowling went to Edinburgh, Scotland, with her infant daughter . . .
Rowling took Jessica on long walks around Edinburgh. When the baby fell asleep,
Rowling stopped at coffee shops to write.

6. Circle the word that is close in meaning to *infant*.

owling sent her book to publishers. It was rejected several times.

7. In other words, the publishers . . .

(A) gave her awards.
(B) chose not to publish her book.
(C) accepted her book.

Rowling has won many awards and is the wealthiest woman in the U.K.

8. Another word for *wealthiest* is . . .

(A) richest.
(B) most famous.
(C) luckiest.

Is it the fast action, the humor , or the magic?

9. A book that is full of *humor* . . .

(A) is easy to read.
(B) makes people think.
(C) is funny.

According to Rowling, it is because "the books are really about the power of the
imagination ."

10. Another word for *imagination* is . . .

(A) intelligence.
(B) creativity.
(C) emotion.

While You Read

Here are six points that are discussed in the reading. There is one point for each paragraph. While you read, put the points in order from 1 to 6.

_____ Rowling's plan for the Harry Potter series
_____ The first idea for the Harry Potter books
_____ The publication of the first Harry Potter book
_____ Rowling's childhood
_____ Rowling's "magical" success
_____ Rowling returns from Portugal and finishes her book

J. K. ROWLING: A MAGICAL AUTHOR

1   Joanne Kathleen Rowling (pronounced *Rolling*) was born in 1966 in Bristol, U.K. From an early age, she enjoyed books. She liked to write stories for her younger sister, Di. Her first story, "Rabbit," was about a rabbit that had the measles.[1] When Rowling was nine, her family moved to a village called Tutshill. Her parents wanted to live in a small town. Rowling loved walking in the woods and by the river with her sister. However, her school was small and old-fashioned. Rowling says that she was shy and was not good at sports. She preferred telling stories.

2   Rowling studied French at Exeter University and then spent a year in Paris. After graduation, she worked as a secretary in London. She says she was "the world's worst secretary." One day, she took a train from Manchester to London. On the trip, she had an idea about a boy who lives with a family that mistreats him. Although the boy doesn't realize it, he is a wizard! Then the boy learns the truth, and he goes to Hogwarts, a school for wizards. By the time Rowling arrived in London, the main characters and the

Fig. 2.2 Harry Potter, played by actor Daniel Radcliffe.

story for her first novel were complete. She also had a name for the hero: Harry Potter.

In 1992, Rowling went to Portugal to teach English. There, she married a Portuguese journalist and had a daughter, Jessica. After her divorce, Rowling went to Edinburgh, Scotland, with her infant daughter and a suitcase full of notes for her novel. She wanted to live near her sister Di. She was unemployed and lived on public assistance.[2] Rowling took Jessica on long walks around Edinburgh. When the baby fell asleep, Rowling stopped at coffee shops to write. That is how she finished her book.

Rowling sent her book to publishers. It was rejected several times. Rowling began teaching French classes. Then she found a literary agent,[3] Christopher Little. She chose Little because she liked his name. He sold her book, which was titled *Harry Potter and the Philosopher's Stone*, to a publishing company in the U.K. (When the book was later published in the U.S., it was called *Harry Potter and the Sorcerer's Stone*.) Rowling then had enough money to quit teaching. She could write all the time.

In her books, Harry attends school at Hogwarts for seven years. Rowling plans to write one novel about each of his school years. Rowling has carefully planned all seven books. In fact, she wrote the final paragraph of the last book before she finished the first book. Her novels have also been made into successful films.

6   Like her famous creation, Harry Potter, J. K. Rowling has had magic in her life. Rowling has sold over one hundred million books. Her books have encouraged young people to read. They are popular with adults too. They have been translated into forty-two languages. Rowling has won many awards and is the wealthiest woman in the U.K.—even wealthier than the Queen. What is the secret of the success of her books? Is it the fast action, the humor, or the magic? According to Rowling, it is because "the books are really about the power of the imagination." Most of her readers agree.

Notes

1. *Measles* is a (usually) minor disease, mainly of children. It causes red spots on the skin.

2. *Public assistance* is money and other aid that governments give to people who are unemployed or have other problems. In some countries, it is called welfare.

3. A *literary agent* helps authors sell their books to publishing companies.

After You Read

❯ Understanding the Reading

Complete these multiple-choice questions to see how well you understood the reading.

1. Why did the Rowling family move to Tutshill?

    (A) Because the schools were good there
    (B) Because Rowling's parents opened a business there
    (C) Because Rowling's parents wanted to live in a small town

2. What did Rowling like to do when she was a girl?

   (A) Play sports
   (B) Read books and tell stories
   (C) Talk to her teacher

3. Where was Rowling going when she got the idea for *Harry Potter?*

   (A) To Portugal
   (B) To London
   (C) To Paris

4. Why did Rowling move to Portugal?

   (A) To teach English
   (B) To study Portuguese
   (C) To work as a journalist

5. Where did Rowling write much of the first Harry Potter book?

   (A) In her small apartment
   (B) On trains
   (C) In coffee shops

6. Rowling chose Christopher Little as her literary agent because . . .

   (A) she liked his name.
   (B) he was very successful with children's books.
   (C) he was an old friend of hers.

7. What is different about the U.K. edition of the first Harry Potter book and the U.S. edition?

   (A) The names of some characters
   (B) The basic story
   (C) The title of the book

8. How many novels will be in the Harry Potter series when Rowling finishes it?

   (A) Five
   (B) Seven
   (C) Twelve

» Vocabulary Building

Fill in the blanks in the sentences below with one of these words from the reading.

magic	wizard	translated	old-fashioned
frightening	shy	wealthiest	novel

1. Do you prefer to read a _____ or a nonfiction book?

2. Merlin the magician is another famous _____ in English literature.

3. A: My brother can do a _____ trick.

   B: Oh really?

   A: Yes, if you give him a snack, he can make it disappear in a few seconds!

4. A: Evelyn's children won't talk to me.

   B: Well, her children seem _____ when you first meet them. But once they get to know you, they won't stop talking.

5. A: Are you and your wife staying in a modern hotel?

   B: No, we like to stay in small, _____ hotels.

6. Gregorio _____ several novels from English into Spanish.

7. Every year, *Forbes Magazine* lists the _____ people in the United States. For the last several years, Bill Gates has been listed as the richest.

8. Thunderstorms are _____ to some children. They hide under their bed covers until the storm is over.

Reading Skill: Understanding Verbs in Readings

Verbs contain a lot of information. The *meaning* of a verb names the action, or the condition of something. The *tense* tells the time it happened.

There are three basic tenses in English: past, present, and future. Each tense has different forms: simple, progressive, and perfect. Each form shows a different kind of time.

The verbs in this reading are mostly simple present, present perfect, and simple past tense verbs. Look at the chart to learn the differences between them.

Note: This is a simple chart that doesn't explain all the uses of these verb tenses.

Simple Present Tense

(A) Shows **habit**
(B) States **facts**
(C) Is used to talk about **art** (novels, paintings, movies, etc.) or an artist or writer's **views**

> Habit: He *stays* at the Chandler Hotel when he is in Los Angeles.
>
> I *take* a shower every morning.
>
> Fact: Sylvie *lives* in Paris.
>
> The sun *rises* in the east.
>
> Art/View: James Bond *is* a secret agent.
>
> Kung Fu-tzu *says* that we must respect other people.

Present Perfect Tense

Used for events that **began sometime in the past, and may continue in the present**

> Mi Son *has been* a journalist for five years.
> Fahar *hasn't finished* the article yet.

Simple Past Tense

(A) Shows **completed actions**
(B) States **past facts**

> Mr. Bhugatra *visited* Sydney in 2002.
> Margarita *was* sick on Thursday.

Exercise: The verbs in these sentences appear in **bold**. Write the name of the tense (simple present, present perfect, or simple past) on the line or lines below each sentence.

Example:

When Rowling **was** nine, her family **moved** to a village called Tutshill.

_____ *simple past* _____   _____ *simple past* _____

1. Rowling **says** that she **was** shy and **was** not good at sports.

    _____   _____   _____

2. Rowling **studied** French at Exeter University and **spent** a year in Paris.

    _____   _____

3. On the trip, she **had** an idea about a boy who **lives** with a family that **mistreats** him.

    _____   _____   _____

4. Although he **doesn't realize** it, he **is** a wizard!

    _____   _____

5. In 1992, Rowling **went** to Portugal.

    _____

6. Rowling **has sold** over one hundred million books.

    _____

7. Her books **have encouraged** young people to read.

    _____

8. They **are** popular with adults too.

    _____

❯ Focus on Listening

Listen to the recording of the reading "J. K. Rowling: A Magical Author." You will hear this reading two times. The first time, read along with the recording. Listen to the sound and tone of the words. The second time, listen for meaning. Do not look at the reading. Try to follow the ideas by listening only.

As you listen the second time, the speaker will stop occasionally and make statements about the reading. Decide if the statements are true or false. Fill in the space of the circled T or F according to what you hear and remember from the reading.

1. (T) (F).   5. (T) (F)

2. (T) (F)   6. (T) (F)

3. (T) (F)   7. (T) (F)

4. (T) (F)   8. (T) (F)

❯ Writing and Discussion Questions

Work with a partner or group to answer these questions.

1. This reading is a biography. In other words, it tells the story of J. K. Rowling's life. Write a short (one paragraph) biography of someone you know. It may be a famous person, a friend, or a relative.

2. Exchange biographies with a classmate. Read your partner's biography and discuss it with him or her. Take notes. Report to the class on what you read.

3. In general, do you prefer to read stories about ordinary people and things, or fantasies such as the Harry Potter books? (*Fantasies* are stories about unbelievable people or things.) Explain your choice.

4. Harry Potter is a wizard, and like all wizards, he has magical powers. For example, he can fly on a broomstick. What magical power would you most like to have? Explain your choice.

5. Do you usually enjoy movies based on books that you have read? Why or why not?

➤ Crossword Puzzle

Complete the puzzle with words from the reading.

Across

1 At first, Harry Potter doesn't realize he is a _____.

6 Rowling attended _____ University.

7 Rowling is the _____ woman in the U.K.

9 _____ is J. K. Rowling's sister.

10 As a girl, Rowling was _____.

11 Rowling's first story was about a _____ with the measles.

Down

2 Rowling's first book was _____ by several publishers.

3 In Rowling's books, Harry's family _____ him.

4 Rowling says that she was the "world's worst _____."

5 Harry attends a school called _____.

8 Rowling is a successful _____.

The World Cup Trophy

Fig. 3.1 Soccer players holding the current World Cup trophy.

Before You Read

❯ Warm-Up Questions

Discuss these questions in pairs or groups. Share your ideas with the class.

1. Is soccer an important sport in your country? Describe what happens when your team plays in World Cup events.

2. Look at the photograph of Pickles on page 30. Try to guess why Pickles' picture appears here. Read paragraph 4 in the reading to find the answer.

≫ Vocabulary Preview

These statements come from the reading "The World Cup Trophy." Read each statement and then answer the questions. Check your answers before you begin the reading.

The World Cup soccer competition is the most popular sports event in the world. Every four years, the whole world focuses on this international tournament.

1. *Focuses on* means . . .

(A) remembers.
(B) pays attention to.
(C) plays.

All soccer fans have the same dream—they want to see their team win the World Cup trophy .

2. A *trophy* is a kind of . . .

(A) prize.
(B) game.
(C) player.

The World Cup tournament has a colorful history, and the World Cup trophy does too.

3. A *colorful* history is . . .

(A) long.
(B) true.
(C) interesting.

The first World Cup trophy was a statue of Nike, the Greek goddess of victory, who holds a bowl over her head.

4. Which of these pictures shows the statue with a *bowl*.

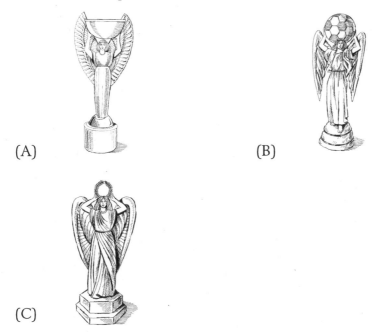

(A)

(B)

(C)

At that time, the trophy was called the Rimet Cup to honor Jules Rimet, president of FIFA from 1921 to 1954.

5. To *honor* is to show . . .

(A) anger.
(B) respect.
(C) happiness.

The Rimet Cup was on display in London.

6. When something is *on display,* people can . . . it.

(A) see
(B) buy
(C) steal

Scotland Yard investigated the crime, but Pickles solved it.

7. Pickles *solved* the crime. In other words, Pickles . . . the crime.

(A) found the answer to
(B) did
(C) planned

Pickles discovered an object that was wrapped in a newspaper and buried in a garden.

8. A *buried* object is . . .

(A) up a tree.
(B) under the ground.
(C) on a table.

World champion teams can no longer keep the actual solid-gold trophy. Instead they receive a smaller copy. The replica is gold-plated , not pure gold.

9. Circle the word that is close in meaning to *replica*.

10. If something is *gold-plated*, it . . .

(A) is 100% gold.
(B) looks like gold but is not real gold.
(C) is covered with a small amount of gold.

While You Read

Here are seven points that are discussed in the reading passage. There is one point for each paragraph. While you read, put the points in order from 1 to 7.

_____ A description of the first World Cup trophy
_____ The first World Cup trophy disappears in Brazil
_____ The popularity of the World Cup tournament
_____ The World Cup trophy today
_____ The first World Cup trophy is stolen and then found in the U.K.
_____ A description of the second World Cup trophy
_____ The World Cup trophy faces danger in World War II

THE WORLD CUP TROPHY

1   The World Cup soccer competition is the most popular sports event in the world. Every four years, the world focuses on this international tournament. In most countries, daily activities stop when the home team plays. All soccer fans have the same dream—they want to see their team win the World Cup trophy.

2   The World Cup tournament has a colorful history, and the World Cup trophy does too. The first World Cup trophy was a statue of Nike, the Greek goddess of victory, who holds a bowl over her head. A French artist, Abel Lafleur, designed it in 1929. It weighed 3.8 kilograms and was 35 centimeters high. It was made of solid gold. Uruguay won this trophy at the first World Cup competition in 1930. At that time, the trophy was called the Rimet Cup to honor Jules Rimet, president of FIFA[1] from 1921 to 1954.

3   The Rimet Cup faced several dangers. During World War II, it was in Italy. Dr. Ottorino Barassi, vice-president of FIFA, kept it safely hidden in a shoebox under his bed.

4   In 1966, the World Cup finals were held in the United Kingdom. The Rimet Cup was on display in London. One day it disappeared. Scotland Yard[2] investigated the crime, but Pickles solved it. Pickles was a small, two-year-old dog. David Corbett was his owner. Two weeks after the robbery, David Corbett and his dog were walking in South London. Pickles discovered an object that was wrapped in a newspaper and buried in a garden. Corbett unwrapped the object. He recognized the trophy and

Fig. 3.2 Pickles.

called the police. Corbett and Pickles received medals, and Pickles was the biggest hero of the 1966 World Cup finals.

In 1970, a new trophy was made. In this year, Brazil won the World Cup for the third time. FIFA rules allowed three-time winners to keep the trophy permanently. Over fifty artists sent in designs for a new trophy. FIFA chose Italian artist Silvio Gazzaniga's design. The new trophy is a statue of two athletes who hold the Earth in their hands. The trophy weighs 5 kilograms and is 36 centimeters high. It is also made of pure gold. The new trophy is called the FIFA World Cup. There are seventeen empty spaces on its base for the names of seventeen champions. FIFA will probably have to create another trophy after the 2038 tournament. There won't be any space for the names of winners after that.

The original 1929 Rimet trophy was in the news again in 1983. The trophy was kept in the headquarters of the Brazilian Soccer Association in Rio de Janeiro. Four men entered the headquarters and stole it. Pele, the Brazilian soccer superstar, went on television to ask the thieves to return the trophy. Some people suggested that Pickles could help find the statue again, but, unfortunately, Pickles had died in 1973. The trophy was never found.

7   Today, FIFA keeps the actual World Cup statue. It is insured for U.S. $23 million. FIFA brings the cup to opening and closing ceremonies, and displays it before the games. During the 2002 tournament, the trophy was displayed in ten Japanese and ten Korean cities. World champion teams can no longer keep the actual solid-gold trophy. Instead, they receive a smaller copy. The replica is gold-plated, not pure gold. However, players and their fans don't really care if the trophy is real or a replica. They just want their dreams of winning the World Cup to come true.

Notes

1. *FIFA* stands for the Fédération Internationale de Football Association, the group that regulates World Cup football.

2. *Scotland Yard* is the headquarters of the police in London.

After You Read

➤ Understanding the Reading

Answer these multiple-choice questions to see how well you understood the reading.

1. Who designed the first World Cup trophy?

   (A) Jules Rimet
   (B) Abel Lafleur
   (C) Silvio Gazzaniga

2. Where was the World Cup trophy during World War II?

   (A) In the FIFA headquarters
   (B) In a newspaper in a garden
   (C) In a shoebox under a bed

3. Who found the World Cup trophy in 1966?

   (A) Pickles
   (B) Pele
   (C) Scotland Yard

4. Which country was allowed to keep the trophy after winning the World Cup finals three times?

    (A) Brazil
    (B) Uruguay
    (C) Mexico

5. Which of these statements about the second World Cup trophy is true?

    (A) It is heavier than the first trophy but not as tall.
    (B) It is taller than the first trophy but not as heavy.
    (C) It is taller and heavier than the first trophy.

6. Why will FIFA need a new trophy in 2038?

    (A) The trophy will probably be stolen again.
    (B) There will be no more spaces for the names of the winners on the trophy.
    (C) One country will keep the trophy after winning the finals three times.

7. What happened to the Rimet trophy in 1983?

    (A) It was stolen and never found.
    (B) It was displayed all over the world.
    (C) It was found after being lost for many years.

8. The World Cup trophy was displayed in how many cities before the 2002 finals?

    (A) Five
    (B) Ten
    (C) Twenty

❯ Vocabulary Building

Fill in the blanks in the sentences below with one of these words from the reading.

tournament	statue	permanently	replica
colorful	buried	unwrapped	unfortunately

Fig. 3.3 *Le Penseur* (The Thinker).

1. Rodin was a French sculptor. His most famous _____ is called *Le Penseur* (The Thinker).

2. Rodin's original sculpture *Le Penseur* is in a museum in France, but I once saw a _____ of this statue in New York City.

3. My grandfather had an exciting life. He told me many _____ stories.

4. There was a big snowstorm last night. This morning, my car was _____ under half a meter of snow.

5. The British Open is a well known golf _____ that is played every year in the U.K.

6. After the wedding, the bride and groom _____ their wedding gifts.

7. George really wanted to go to the soccer game on Saturday. _____, he had to work that day.

8. Mr. Choi does not plan to move to Madrid _____. He will be there only for six months.

Reading Skill: Understanding Pronoun Reference

A pronoun is a word that takes the place of a noun.

Francesca is a soccer fan. *She* loves to go to games.

The pronoun *She* refers to *Francesca*. These sentences mean, "Francesca is a soccer fan. Francesca loves to go to games."

When you are reading, it is important to understand which noun a pronoun refers to.

Here are some points to remember about English pronouns:

- A masculine pronoun (*he, him, his, himself*) refers to a single male (*a man, James, a boy, Mr. Jones*).

- A feminine pronoun (*she, her, hers, herself*) refers to a single female (*a woman, an actress, Francesca*) or thing spoken of as female (*a ship, a statue of woman*).

- A neuter pronoun (*it, its, itself*) refers to a single thing or idea (*a bicycle, a house, soccer, truth*).

- A plural pronoun (*they, them, their, theirs, themselves*) can refer to plural males, females, things, or ideas (*bicycles, actresses, boys, soccer balls*).

- An animal is usually referred to as *it*, but a pet, such as a dog or a cat, is usually *he* or *she*.

- A pronoun almost always comes AFTER the noun that it refers to.

Exercise: Here are some sentences from the reading. Read each sentence, and then answer the questions about pronoun reference.

In most countries, daily activities stop when the home team plays. All soccer fans have the same dream—they want to see their team win the World Cup trophy.

1. The pronoun *their* refers to . . .

(A) most countries.
(B) everyday activities.
(C) the home team.
(D) all soccer fans.

The first World Cup trophy was a statue of Nike, the Greek goddess of victory, who holds a bowl over her head.

2. The pronoun *her* refers to . . .

(A) the statue of Nike.
(B) the bowl.

Pickles was a small, two-year old dog. David Corbett was his owner.

3. The word *his* refer to . . .

(A) Pickles.
(B) David Corbett.

Two weeks after the robbery, David Corbett and his dog were walking in South London.

4. The word *his* refers to . . .

(A) the dog.
(B) Corbett.
(C) South London.

The new trophy is a statue of two athletes who hold the Earth in their hands.

5. The word *their* refers to . . .

(A) two athletes.
(B) hands.

Today, FIFA keeps the actual World Cup statue. It is insured for U.S. $23 million.

6. The pronoun *it* refers to . . .

(A) FIFA.
(B) the world.
(C) the World Cup statue.

However, players and their fans don't really care if the trophy is real or a replica.

7. The pronoun *their* refers to . . .

(A) players.
(B) fans.

➤ Focus on Listening

Listen to the recording of the reading "The World Cup Trophy." You will hear this reading two times. The first time, read along with the recording. Listen to the sound and tone of the words. The second time, listen for meaning. Do not look at the reading. Try to follow the ideas by listening only.

As you listen the second time, the speaker will stop occasionally and make statements about the reading. Decide if the statements are true or false. Fill in the space of the circled T or F according to what you hear and remember from the reading.

1. Ⓣ Ⓕ   5. Ⓣ Ⓕ

2. Ⓣ Ⓕ   6. Ⓣ Ⓕ

3. Ⓣ Ⓕ   7. Ⓣ Ⓕ

4. Ⓣ Ⓕ   8. Ⓣ Ⓕ

➤ Writing and Discussion Questions

Work with a partner or group to answer these questions.

1. Imagine these two choices: You can go to the World Cup finals or take a vacation at the beach. Which would you prefer to do? Why?

2. Do you prefer to play games such as soccer or to watch them? Explain your answer.

3. These are the names of some other important sports trophies. Using the Internet, get some basic information about three of them. Find out in what sport the trophy is given, the year it was first given, and other basic facts. Write several sentences about each trophy. If possible, try to find a picture of the trophy. Share the information that you find with your class.

Ryder Cup   Thomas Cup
Vince Lombardi Trophy   Stanley Cup
Davis Cup   America's Cup
Borg-Warner Cup   Leonard Trophy

❯ Crossword Puzzle

Complete the puzzle with words from the reading.

Across

3 Scotland _____ investigates crimes in London.

6 The first World Cup trophy was a statue of the goddess _____.

7 When the trophy was stolen in Brazil, the crime was never _____.

9 The first World Cup trophy was named to _____ a president of FIFA.

11 _____ found the first World Cup trophy in a garden.

12 _____ organizes the World Cup finals.

13 The first World Cup trophy was called the _____ Cup.

Down

1 The first World Cup trophy was a statue of a goddess holding a _____.

2 _____ was a great Brazilian soccer star.

4 The trophy was _____ in a garden by a dog.

5 Corbett _____ the object and found the trophy.

8 The trophy was on _____ in London when it was stolen.

10 The dog found the trophy _____ in a garden.

The Pizza Story

Fig. 4.1 People eating pizza in the 1950s.

Before You Read

Warm-Up Questions

Discuss these questions in pairs or groups. Share your ideas with the class.

1. Do you enjoy pizza? Why or why not?

2. Does everyone like the same kind of pizza? What do you think? Look at the reading to find out.

❯ Vocabulary Preview

These statements come from the reading "The Pizza Story." Read each statement and then answer the questions. Check your answers before you begin the reading.

It can have a thick crust or a thin one.

1. Circle the word that is the opposite of *thick*.

They covered them with all kinds of ingredients , such as olive oil, herbs, and meat.

2. *Ingredients* are . . .

    (A) foods used to make a dish.
    (B) materials to keep food warm.
    (C) spices to make food taste hot.

At first, Europeans thought that tomatoes were poisonous , but soon they were an important part of Italian cooking.

3. *Poisonous* foods . . .

    (A) are vegetables.
    (B) make people sick or die.
    (C) are delicious.

They carried their pizzas in metal ovens on their heads.

4. The main purpose of *ovens* is to . . .

    (A) cook or heat foods.
    (B) attract people's attention.
    (C) keep people's heads warm.

In the 1890s, Italian immigrants brought pizza to the United States.

5. What are *immigrants*?

    (A) Cooks, waiters, and other restaurant workers
    (B) Tourists and other travelers
    (C) People who come to live permanently in another country

At first, pizza was mostly sold in Italian neighborhoods in big cities.

6. *Neighborhoods* are . . .

   (A) small restaurants.
   (B) sections of a city.
   (C) outdoor markets.

In the late 1940s and 1950s, interest in pizza exploded . A line from a song by Italian-American singer Dean Martin—"When the moon hits your eye like a big pizza pie, that's *amore*"—got people's attention .

7. If interest in something *exploded,* it . . .

   (A) slowly increased.
   (B) stopped suddenly.
   (C) grew quickly.

8. Find and circle another word that means *attention.*

Most of these were small restaurants that were owned by families, but soon there were large chains of pizza restaurants—Shakey's, Pizza Hut, Dominos, and others.

9. Restaurant *chains* are . . .

   (A) groups of similar restaurants that are owned by one company.
   (B) restaurants that steal ideas from other restaurants.
   (C) large restaurants for hundreds or even thousands of people.

It doesn't matter what people put on it, though, it's all pizza!

10. If something *doesn't matter,* it isn't . . .

   (A) true.
   (B) known.
   (C) important.

While You Read

Here are six points that are discussed in the reading passage. There is one point for each paragraph. While you read, put the points in order from 1 to 6.

_____ The origin of the first pizza
_____ Pizza toppings around the world
_____ An introduction to different types of pizza
_____ Two ingredients needed for modern pizza
_____ Pizza comes to the United States
_____ Naples becomes the center of pizza

THE PIZZA STORY

1   It is eaten almost everywhere. It can be served with all kinds of toppings and sauces. It can have a thick crust or a thin one. It can be round or square, frozen or fresh. It's pizza, one of the world's favorite foods.

2   Pizza came from the eastern Mediterranean, from Greece, Egypt, and Turkey. People there cooked flat breads on hot stones. They covered them with all kinds of ingredients, such as olive oil, herbs, and meat. This was a popular food because it was easy to eat without a knife and fork or even a plate. The bread itself was the plate. Roman soldiers brought this food back to Italy.

3   However, two ingredients were needed to make modern pizza. Tomatoes first came to Italy from South America in the sixteenth century. At first, Europeans thought that tomatoes were poisonous, but soon they were an important part of Italian cooking. The other important ingredient was mozzarella cheese.[1] This cheese was originally made from the milk of water buffalos.

Fig. 4.2 Man making pizza in nineteenth-century Italy.

Mozzarella was introduced to Italy from India in the eighteenth century.

Naples became the pizza center of Italy. Men called *pizzaioli* walked around town selling pizza. They carried their pizzas in metal ovens on their heads. In 1830, people ate pizzas in a restaurant for the first time. That's when Antica Pizzeria Port'Alba, the world's first pizza restaurant, opened its doors.

In the 1890s, Italian immigrants brought pizza to the United States. Gennaro Lombardi opened the first U.S. pizza restaurant on Spring Street in New York City. At first, pizza was mostly sold in Italian neighborhoods in big cities. However, during and after World War II, many U.S. soldiers spent time in Italy and learned to love pizza. They brought their taste for pizza home with them. In the late 1940s and 1950s, interest in pizza exploded. A line from a song by Italian-American singer Dean Martin—"When the moon hits your eye like a big pizza pie,[2] that's *amore*"[3]—got people's attention. Thousands of pizza restaurants opened around the country. Most of these were small restaurants that were owned by families, but soon there were large chains of pizza restaurants—Shakeys, Pizza Hut, Dominos, and others. Pizza lovers could also enjoy pizza at home. Bake-at-home pizzas were first sold in 1948, and frozen pizzas were first sold in 1957.

6

Fig. 4.3 Preparing toppings for pizza in Hong Kong.

From the United States, pizza spread around the world. The basic recipe for pizza is similar everywhere, but different countries enjoy different sauces and especially toppings. In the United States, the favorite topping is pepperoni, but in the U.K., it is chicken. In Pakistan, curry is a favorite, and Brazilians like green peas. Australians like shrimp and pineapple on their pies, Costa Ricans favor coconut, and Russians enjoy smoked fish. It doesn't matter what people put on it, though, it's all pizza!

Notes

1. *Mozzarella cheese* is a white, mild cheese that is often used on pizza and in other Italian dishes.

2. *Pizza pie* is another way to say pizza.

3. *Amore* is the Italian word for *love*.

After You Read

❯ Understanding the Reading

Answer these multiple-choice questions to see how well you understood the reading.

1. Which sequence correctly shows the spread of pizza?

   (A) Italy ➔ the Eastern Mediterranean ➔ the United States ➔ the rest of the world

   (B) The United States ➔ the U.K. ➔ Pakistan ➔ Brazil ➔ Australia ➔ Costa Rica ➔ Russia

   (C) The eastern Mediterranean ➔ Italy ➔ the United States ➔ the rest of the world

2. Why was pizza popular in ancient times?

   (A) Because it was easy to make
   (B) Because people didn't need a plate or a knife and fork to eat it
   (C) Because it was inexpensive

3. What did people in Europe first think of the tomato?

   (A) It was dangerous to eat.
   (B) It was very nutritious.
   (C) It had a strange taste.

4. Where did mozzarella cheese originally come from?

   (A) The countries of the eastern Mediterranean
   (B) South America
   (C) India

5. In Naples, *pizzaioli* were . . .

   (A) small pizzas.
   (B) people who sold pizza.
   (C) restaurants that served only pizza.

6. Why is Dean Martin mentioned in paragraph 5?

   (A) He sang about pizza in a very popular song.
   (B) He opened a popular pizza restaurant.
   (C) He was a U.S. soldier during World War II.

7. When were frozen pizzas first sold?

   (A) In 1890
   (B) In 1948
   (C) In 1957

8. What is the most popular topping on pizza in the U.K.?

   (A) Curry
   (B) Pepperoni
   (C) Chicken

❯ Vocabulary Building

Part 1: Fill in the blanks

Fill in the blanks in the sentences below with one of these words from the reading.

ingredients	originally	chains	spread
poisonous	served	frozen	recipe

Fig. 4.4 A card from the game Pokemon.

Fig. 4.5 Mushrooms.

1. A: Where is Mr. Eubanks from?

   B: He is _____ from Jamaica, but now he lives in London.

2. Italian ice is my favorite kind of _____ dessert. I like it better than ice cream.

3. Pokemon games and cartoons began in Japan, but soon their popularity _____ all over the world.

4. Best Western, Hilton, Hyatt, Marriott: these are some of the world's largest hotel _____.

5. A: Do you like this spaghetti sauce?

   B: It's wonderful. In fact, I'd like you to give me the _____ for it.

   A: The main _____ for this sauce are tomatoes, mushrooms, peppers, and garlic.

6. Some mushrooms are _____, but most of them are harmless.

7. In some restaurants, bread is _____ with olive oil instead of with butter.

Part 2: Matching

In the reading, there are several words that refer to the parts of pizza. Below is a simple picture of a pizza. Match the number of the arrow with the correct word.

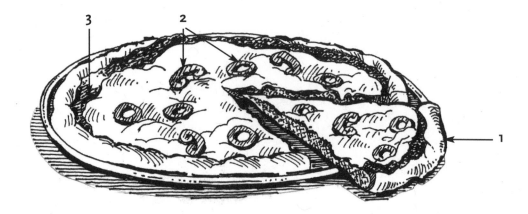

_____ (A) Topping

_____ (B) Crust

_____ (C) Sauce

Reading Skill: Skimming 1

Skimming is an important reading skill. When you skim, you read quickly to find the topic or main idea. You can skim a paragraph, an article, a web page, a textbook chapter, or a whole book. You skim if you are in a hurry, if you have a lot to read, or if you need to review.

There are four basic rules for skimming.

- Read about three to four times faster than your normal reading speed.

- Don't try to understand more than about 50% of the material.

- Don't worry about vocabulary that you don't understand.

- Don't pay attention to details (See Unit 5, page 58).

There are many ways to skim. One basic way is by quickly finding and reading the summary sentences (See Unit 1, page 8).

Exercise: Skim the reading below in three to four minutes. Then answer the question that follows. Mark your beginning time and ending time.

Beginning time: _____

In 1889, Umberto I, king of Italy, and his wife Margherita, queen of Savoy, visited Naples. They stayed at a palace that belonged to the queen's family. Queen Margherita had heard of the wonderful pizza that was made in Naples. She asked Rafaele Esposito to come to the palace. Esposito was the chef at the best pizza restaurant in Naples, Pizzeria Brandi. She asked him to make a pizza for her and her husband.

Esposito prepared a new type of pizza just for the queen. To make it patriotic, he used the colors of the Italian flag: tomatoes (red), mozzarella cheese (white), and herbs (green). He brought it to the palace. This was probably the world's first home delivery of pizza.

The queen loved this new type of pizza. She sent a thank-you letter to the chef. This letter can still be seen on the wall in the Pizzeria Brandi. To honor the queen, Esposito named this type of pizza "Pizza Margherita." It became the most popular style of pizza in Naples. Pizza Margherita also became the basic model for the modern pizza.

Ending time: _____

What is this reading mainly about?

(A) The design of the Italian flag
(B) The story of King Umberto and Queen Margherita
(C) The creation of the basic model for modern pizza
(D) The history of Pizzeria Brandi

❯❯ Focus on Listening

Listen to the recording of the reading "The Pizza Story." You will hear this reading two times. The first time, read along with the recording. Listen to the sound and tone of the words. The second time, listen for meaning. Do not look at the reading. Try to follow the ideas by listening only.

As you listen the second time, the speaker will stop occasionally and make statements about the reading. Decide if the statements are true or false. Fill in the space of the circled T or F according to what you hear and remember from the reading.

1. ⓉⒻ   5. ⓉⒻ

2. ⓉⒻ   6. ⓉⒻ

3. ⓉⒻ   7. ⓉⒻ

4. ⓉⒻ   8. ⓉⒻ

❯❯ Writing and Discussion Questions

Work with a partner or group to answer these questions.

1. Describe the first pizza you ever ate. How old were you? Where were you? What were the ingredients?

2. Interview one of your classmates. Ask your classmate to describe his or her perfect pizza. Then ask your classmate to name some toppings he or she finds unusual on pizza. Then report to the class on what you learned from your classmate.

3. Pizza is a popular food almost all over the world. Describe some other popular foods in your country. Are these foods originally from your country or are they international foods?

≫ Crossword Puzzle

Complete the puzzle with words from the reading.

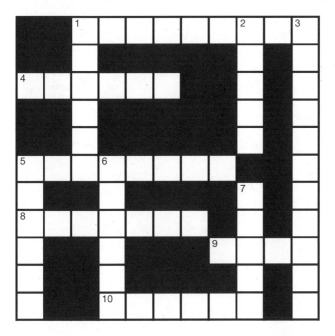

Across

1 The most popular pizza topping in the United States is _____.

4 Pizza Hut and Dominos are large pizza _____.

5 _____ enjoy smoked fish on their pizzas.

8 In Costa Rica, _____ is a popular topping.

9 In his song, Dean Martin compares the _____ to a pizza.

10 Pizzas can be round or _____.

Down

1 You can eat pizza without knives, forks, or _____.

2 Street salesmen in Naples carried their pizzas in metal _____ on their heads.

3 Mozzarella cheese and tomatoes are two important pizza _____.

5 The basic _____ for pizza is similar all over the world.

6 In ancient times, pizzas were baked on hot _____.

7 The Italian word for *love* is _____.

Australia's Living Teddy Bears

Fig. 5.1 A koala.

Before You Read

» Warm-Up Questions

Discuss these questions in pairs or groups. Share your ideas with the class.

1. Look at the photo and the title of the reading. What will this reading be about?

2. The reading says that "koalas are among the world's favorite animals." What is your favorite animal? Tell why, and describe it to the class.

❯ Vocabulary Preview

These statements come from the reading "Australia's Living Teddy Bears." Read each statement and then answer the questions. Check your answers before you begin the reading.

But how much do you know about these charming little animals?

1. A *charming* animal is . . .

   (A) weak.
   (B) attractive.
   (C) rare.

They look like blind , pink worms.

2. An animal that is *blind* is . . .

   (A) tiny.
   (B) unable to see.
   (C) helpless.

Koalas' large, sensitive noses help them pick the best leaves.

3. An animal with a *sensitive* nose . . .

   (A) has a very good sense of smell.
   (B) cannot smell anything.
   (C) has a very long nose.

Koalas are nocturnal animals. They are active mainly at twilight .

4. *Twilight* is . . .

   (A) early morning.
   (B) evening.
   (C) late night.

Koalas are well adapted to life in trees.

5. Animals that are *well adapted* to life in trees . . .

   (A) climb trees only to escape danger.
   (B) never climb trees.
   (C) are comfortable in trees.

They have two thumbs on each of their four paws. This helps them grip branches.

6. To *grip* branches means to . . . them.

   (A) climb
   (B) chew
   (C) hold

Koalas come out of trees only to get to other trees, and they are clumsy on the ground.

7. An animal that is *clumsy* . . .

   (A) doesn't move easily or fast.
   (B) cannot be seen.
   (C) is confused and afraid.

In 1921 alone, Australia exported two million koala furs.

8. What did Australians do with the koala furs?

   (A) Traded them to other countries
   (B) Wore them
   (C) Purchased them from other countries

Domestic dogs attack them, and cars hit them when they cross roads.

9. *Domestic* dogs are dogs that . . .

   (A) are extremely hungry.
   (B) live in houses with people.
   (C) are wild and savage.

More than 75% of the koalas' habitat is now gone.

10. A *habitat* is an animal's . . .

   (A) natural enemies.
   (B) food supply.
   (C) home.

While You Read

Here are eight points that are discussed in the reading. There is one point for each paragraph. While you read, put the points in order from 1 to 8.

_____ Birth and growth of koalas
_____ Dangers that koalas face
_____ Koalas' territories
_____ Koalas' classification, habitat, and other names
_____ What koalas look like
_____ Koalas' activities and life in trees
_____ The possibility of extinction for koalas
_____ Koalas' food

AUSTRALIA'S LIVING TEDDY BEARS

1   Everyone loves koala bears. With their gray and white fur, round ears, big noses, and small black eyes, they look like teddy bears.[1] Koalas are among the world's favorite animals. But how much do you know about these charming little animals?

2   Koalas are not really bears. They are marsupials.[2] They live in Australia, mostly in the provinces of New South Wales and Queensland. They have several other names: bangaroos, New Holland sloths, and Australian bears.

3   Baby koalas, like baby kangaroos, are called joeys. Female koalas usually have one baby at a time. Twins are rare. Baby koalas can't open their eyes. They look like blind, pink worms. Joeys stay in their mothers' pouches. At six months, joeys look out of their mothers' pouches. At seven months, they ride on their mothers' backs. Male koalas grow to about 85 centimeters in length and weigh 12 kilograms; females are a little smaller.

Fig. 5.2 A koala in a eucalyptus tree.

4   Koalas spend a lot of time eating. They eat only the leaves of eucalyptus trees.[3] However, they cannot eat all eucalyptus leaves. The leaves of some trees are poisonous, and some have an unpleasant taste. Koalas' large, sensitive noses help them pick the best leaves. The leaves give the koala all the water they need. In fact, the name *koala*, which comes from one of the languages of the Aborigines,[4] means *no drink*.

5   Koalas are nocturnal animals.[5] They are active mainly at twilight. During the day and for most of the night, they sleep in trees. Because their diet of leaves is low in protein, they sleep 80% of their lives. Koalas are well adapted to life in trees. They have sharp claws on their paws to help them climb. They have two thumbs on each of their four paws. This helps them grip branches. Koalas come out of trees only to get to other trees, and they are clumsy on the ground.

6   Except for mothers and joeys, koalas live alone. Each has a home territory. The territory is a fairly large section of forest, but the koala regularly uses only a few trees in the territory. In fact, a koala may spend 30% of its time in one favorite tree. Male koalas growl loudly when other males come into their territories.

7

Fig. 5.3 A "Koala Crossing" road sign.

Before Europeans came to Australia, Aborigines hunted koalas for food. Dingoes, the wild dogs of Australia, hunted them too. Over time, Aborigines changed their diet and the number of dingoes decreased, but there was a new danger. European Australians started to hunt koalas for their warm fur. Because koalas are friendly and slow-moving, they were easy to hunt. In 1921 alone, Australia exported two million koala furs. Today, they are protected from hunters, but they still face many dangers. Domestic dogs attack them, and cars hit them when they cross roads. Other threats are forest fires and diseases. However, the biggest danger is the destruction of the eucalyptus forests. More than 75% of the koalas' habitat is now gone.

8

Koalas are not now on the list of endangered species. However, some animal experts believe that the koala is in danger of extinction. They fear that in a decade or two, these "living teddy bears" may be seen only at zoos.

Notes

1. *Teddy bears* are stuffed toys that look like friendly bears. Young children love teddy bears.

2. *Marsupials* are a type of animal. A female marsupial keeps her baby in a pouch for the first few months of the baby's life. The kangaroo is a well-known marsupial.

3. *Eucalyptus trees* are tall trees native to Australia. Eucalyptus leaves have an oil that gives them a strong smell.

4. *Aborigines* are the original people of Australia. They lived there many centuries before the arrival of European Australians.

5. *Nocturnal animals* are active at night.

After You Read

❯ Understanding the Reading

Answer these multiple-choice questions to see how well you understood the reading.

1. Which is NOT another name for a koala?

   (A) Australian bears
   (B) Bangaroos
   (C) Queensland teddies

2. What do baby koalas first do at the age of seven months?

   (A) Look out of their mothers' pouches
   (B) Drink milk
   (C) Ride on their mothers' backs

3. Which of these koalas are the largest?

   (A) Adult males
   (B) Adult females
   (C) Joeys

4. Which statement about eucalyptus leaves is NOT true?

   (A) Some taste bad to koalas.
   (B) Some make koalas thirsty.
   (C) Some are poisonous to koalas.

5. How many thumbs does every koala have?

   (A) Two
   (B) Four
   (C) Eight

6. Why do koalas come out of trees?

   (A) To meet other koalas
   (B) To get to other trees
   (C) To look for water

7. What do koalas do most of the night?

(A) Sleep
(B) Travel around their territories
(C) Eat

8. Which of these dangers did koalas face first?

(A) European Australians hunted them for their fur.
(B) Cars hit them when they tried to cross roads.
(C) Dingoes and Aborigines hunted them for food.

≫ Vocabulary Building

Fill in the blanks in the sentences below with one of these words from the reading.

unpleasant	sensitive	domestic	grip
clumsy	cross	twilight	endangered

1. Marie-Claire has very _____ hearing. She can hear sounds that no one else can hear.

2. A: Why don't you ask Natasha to dance?

    B: I'm so _____, I'll probably step on her toes.

3. The bridge was destroyed, so they had to _____ the river somewhere else.

4. My favorite time of day is _____, just before dark.

5. The word _____ can mean the opposite of *wild*. It can also mean the opposite of *international*.

6. A: I like the smell of pipe smoke.

    B: Really? Not me. I think any kind of smoke is _____.

7. An _____ animal faces extinction.

8. Ken didn't have a good _____ on his golf club. When he took a swing, the club flew through the air.

Reading Skill: Distinguishing Main Ideas and Details

Main ideas are the important ideas, the general ideas of a reading or a paragraph (see Unit 1, page 8).

Details are specific pieces of information. Details are used to support main ideas, to provide examples, or simply to make a reading more interesting.

Exercise: Following are some main ideas and some details of the reading. Mark the main ideas **MI** and the details **D**.

_____ 1. Koalas are popular animals.

_____ 2. Koala mothers seldom have twins.

_____ 3. Female koalas are slightly smaller than males.

_____ 4. Some eucalyptus leaves have an unpleasant taste to koalas.

_____ 5. Koalas are suited to life in trees.

_____ 6. Koalas have two thumbs on each of their paws.

_____ 7. Koalas face many dangers.

_____ 8. Australia exported over two million koala furs in 1921.

» Focus on Listening

Listen to the recording of the reading "Australia's Living Teddy Bears." You will hear this reading two times. The first time, read along with the recording. Listen to the sound and tone of the words. The second time, listen for meaning. Do not look at the reading. Try to follow the ideas by listening only.

As you listen the second time, the speaker will stop occasionally and make statements about the reading. Decide if the statements are true or false. Fill in the space of the circled T or F according to what you hear and remember from the reading.

1. (T) (F)   5. (T) (F)

2. (T) (F)   6. (T) (F)

3. (T) (F)   7. (T) (F)

4. (T) (F)   8. (T) (F)

❯ Writing and Discussion Questions

Work with a partner or group to answer these questions.

1. Use the Internet to identify some other animals that are in danger of extinction. How can we protect them?

2. Here is a list of other animals that live only in Australia. Use the Internet to learn some basic information about two of them. Try to find pictures of the animal that you choose. Write several sentences about each of the animals that you choose. Share the information that you find with the class.

bandicoot	kookaburra	sugar glider	Tasmanian devil
emu	wallaby	cassowary	frilled neck lizard
numbat	dingo	kangaroo	platypus

3. Many koalas were killed for their fur. Some people today believe that it is cruel to kill animals for their fur. What is your opinion?

➤ Crossword Puzzle

Complete the puzzle with words from the reading.

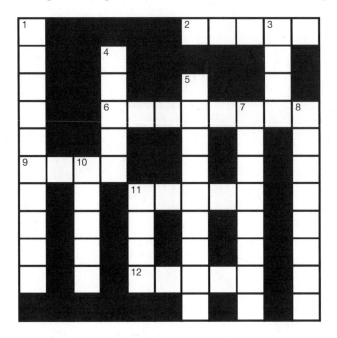

Across

2 Koalas' _____ claws help them climb trees.

6 In the 1920s, Australia _____ koala furs.

9 Koalas have two thumbs on each of their _____.

11 Male koalas _____ when another male comes into their territories.

12 A baby koala first lives in its mother's _____.

Down

1 Koalas are classified as _____.

3 Twins are _____ among koalas.

4 Baby koalas are called _____.

5 Some eucalyptus leaves are _____ to koalas.

7 Koalas are most active at _____.

8 _____ dogs are a danger to koalas.

10 Koalas live mostly in Queensland and New South _____.

11 Koalas' thumbs help them _____ branches.

The Power of the Wind

Fig. 6.1 A wind farm.

Before You Read

❯ Warm-Up Questions

Discuss this question in pairs or groups. Share your ideas with the class.

1. Look at the photograph. What is a wind farm?

2. What are some advantages and disadvantages of wind power? Look quickly at paragraphs 5 and 6 of the reading for ideas.

❯ Vocabulary Preview

These statements come from the reading "The Power of the Wind." Read each statement and then answer the questions. Check your answers before you begin the reading.

Gentle breezes help us fly kites in spring and cool us in summer. The strong winds of hurricanes, typhoons, and tornadoes destroy lives and property.

1. Circle the phrase that is OPPOSITE in meaning to *gentle breezes*.

2. *Hurricanes, typhoons,* and *tornadoes* are examples of . . .

   (A) gentle winds.
   (B) destructive wind storms.
   (C) kites.

In the seventeenth century, the people of the Netherlands built windmills to pump seawater.

3. To *pump* water is to . . . it.

   (A) move
   (B) clean
   (C) store

Nowadays , we can use the wind to make electricity.

4. *Nowadays* means . . .

   (A) at present.
   (B) sometimes.
   (C) in the future.

The wind spins the blades of the turbine.

5. If the wind *spins* something, the wind . . .

   (A) moves it up and down.
   (B) damages it.
   (C) turns it around and around.

Wind farms are usually placed in fields, but some are on platforms in the sea where the wind is strong and steady .

6. If wind is *steady*, it blows . . .

(A) extremely hard.
(B) all the time at about the same speed.
(C) only at certain times.

Unlike nuclear energy, it does not create toxic wastes.

7. *Toxic* means . . .

(A) useless.
(B) invisible.
(C) poisonous.

However, the farmers can still raise crops and animals on their farms.

8. Crops are . . .

(A) chickens and ducks.
(B) food plants.
(C) children.

One drawback is that turbines and steel towers are expensive to buy and build. . . . A second disadvantage is noise pollution.

9. Circle the word that has the same meaning as *drawback*.

Denmark's wind energy program is the most ambitious .

10. An *ambitious* program . . .

(A) is not very successful.
(B) lasts for a long time.
(C) has high goals.

While You Read

Here are seven points that are discussed in the reading. There is one point for each paragraph. While you read, put the points in order from 1 to 7.

_____ The history of wind power
_____ The disadvantages of wind power
_____ Wind farms
_____ The advantages of wind power
_____ A description of wind turbine machines
_____ A general look at wind
_____ Wind power around the world

THE POWER OF THE WIND

1   Gentle breezes help us fly kites in spring and cool us in summer. The strong winds of hurricanes, typhoons, and tornadoes destroy lives and property. Winds can be friendly or dangerous. They can also work for us.

2   Wind power is not new. Five thousand years ago, the Chinese used windmills. In A.D. 700, the Syrians and Persians used them too. In the seventeenth century, the people of the Netherlands built windmills to pump seawater. Nowadays, we can use the wind to make electricity.

3   In many countries of the world, wind turbines are very common. A wind turbine is a simple machine that makes electricity. The turbines are placed on steel towers that are 10 to 85 meters high. The wind spins the blades of the turbine. The blades turn a generator to make electricity. A cable takes the electricity to homes, factories, and schools.

4   A group of turbines is called a *wind farm*. Some wind farms have only a few turbines; some have hundreds. Wind farms are usually placed in fields, but some are on platforms in the sea where the wind is strong and steady.

5   Wind energy has several advantages. One advantage is that there will always be wind, but there is only a limited amount of oil, coal, and gas. Wind power is also a clean form of energy. It does not make gases that cause air pollution. Unlike nuclear energy, it does not create toxic wastes. Farmers like wind power because electric companies pay them to use their land. However, the farmers can still raise crops and animals on their farms.

6   Wind power also has some disadvantages. One drawback is that turbines and steel towers are expensive to buy and build. However, the cost has gone down in recent years. A second disadvantage is noise pollution. This was a greater problem in the past than it is now. Today, if you stand under a turbine, you hear only a soft "swoosh, swoosh" sound, like waves at a beach. At a distance of 100 meters, you won't hear turbines at all. For some people, a third disadvantage is visual pollution, but other people like the sight of turbines turning together. Some wind farms are now tourist sites.

7   Today, Spain, Germany, the United States, India, and Denmark are the largest producers of energy from wind. Denmark's wind energy program is the most ambitious. Denmark gets 20% of its energy from wind. Wind power is growing fast. Four times more energy comes from wind now than it did five years ago. Perhaps one day, all countries will use this safe, clean method to make electricity.

After You Read

❯ Understanding the Reading

Answer these multiple-choice questions to see how well you understood the reading.

1. Where were windmills first used?

   (A) In the Netherlands
   (B) In China
   (C) In Syria and Persia

2. How tall are the tallest wind turbine towers likely to be?

   (A) 10 meters
   (B) 85 meters
   (C) 100 meters

3. What is the purpose of the cable in a wind turbine?

   (A) To take electricity to users
   (B) To control the blades
   (C) To provide power for the generator

4. The reading does NOT mention wind farms in which of these locations?

   (A) In fields
   (B) On mountains
   (C) On platforms in the sea

5. What advantage does wind power have over nuclear energy?

   (A) Wind power is much cheaper.
   (B) Nuclear power is limited, but wind power is not.
   (C) Wind power does not produce dangerous wastes.

6. How many disadvantages of wind power does the reading mention?

   (A) Two
   (B) Three
   (C) Four

7. What does the author compare the sound of wind turbines to?

   (A) Ocean waves
   (B) A person's soft voice
   (C) Gentle winds

8. Which country produces the highest percentage of its energy from the wind?

(A) Spain
(B) India
(C) Denmark

≫ Vocabulary Building

Part 1: Fill in the blanks

Fill in the blanks in the sentences below with one of these words from the reading.

breezes   pump   spins   steady
toxic   crops   drawback   ambitious

Fig. 6.2 The Earth.

1. The three most important _____ in my country are wheat, corn, and barley.

2. Cool ocean _____ keep this town comfortable in the summer.

3. The purpose of the heart is to _____ blood through the body.

4. Ms. Loc owns one restaurant now, but she has an _____ plan to open four more restaurants this year.

5. The planet Earth _____ on its axis. This causes day and night.

6. The doctor said that Marc's heartbeat was strong and _____.

7. The factory spilled some _____ chemicals into the river that killed the fish.

8. A: Do you like my plan?

   B: Yes, but it has one major _____. It's far too expensive.

Part 2: Matching

Below is a simple diagram of a wind turbine. It has a *blade, generator, cable,* and *tower.* Try to match the number of the arrows with the correct part.

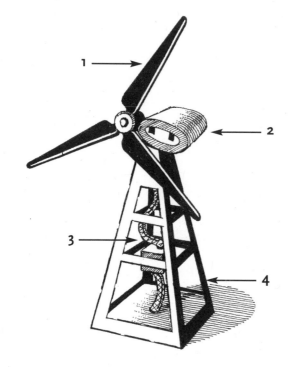

_____ (A) Cable

_____ (B) Blade

_____ (C) Tower

_____ (D) Generator

Reading Skill: Finding the Right Meaning of Words

Sometimes when you read a passage, you find a word that you do not know. When you look it up in the dictionary, you find that the word has two, three, or more meanings. How do you decide which one best fits the passage?

The *context* can help you find the answer. In other words, the information around your unknown word can tell you which definition is correct.

Exercise: Below are sentences from the reading. Read each one, and use the context to guess the meaning of the highlighted words. Put an **X** by the best definition of the word.

Example

Mr. Jones owns land and other property in the city.

property ___X___ (A) (noun) land or other possessions

_____ (B) (noun) a quality; a characteristic

In many countries of the world, wind turbines are very common .

1. common _____ (A) (adjective) shared; the same

_____ (B) (adjective) rude; impolite

_____ (C) (adjective) usual; ordinary

The wind spins the blades of the turbine.

2. blades _____ (A) (noun) parts of a machine such as a fan or an airplane propeller

_____ (B) (noun) the sharp parts of knives

Wind farms are usually placed in fields , but some are on platforms in the sea where the wind is strong and steady.

3. fields _____ (A) (noun) academic subjects

_____ (B) (noun) open areas; land with no trees or buildings

_____ (C) (noun) places to play sports

Farmers like wind power because electric companies pay them to use their land . However, they can still raise crops and animals on their farms.

4. land _____ (A) (noun) nation; country

_____ (B) (noun) property; real estate; part of the Earth's surface

_____ (C) (verb) arrive

5. raise _____ (A) (verb) lift up

_____ (B) (verb) take care of; nurture; bring up

_____ (C) (verb) increase; make bigger

Wind power is also a clean form of energy.

6. form   _____ (A) (noun) a shape, such as a triangle

                      _____ (B) (noun) a document

                      _____ (C) (noun) a type; a kind

                      _____ (D) (verb) create; make; shape

Today, if you stand under a turbine, you hear only a soft "swoosh, swoosh" sound.

7. soft   _____ (A) (adjective) gentle; not loud

                      _____ (B) (adjective) not firm or hard

Denmark's wind energy program is the most ambitious .

8. ambitious _____ (A) (adjective) needing a lot of work or effort

                      _____ (B) (adjective) having a great desire to be wealthy or famous

❯ Focus on Listening

Listen to the recording of the reading "The Power of the Wind." You will hear this reading two times. The first time, read along with the recording. Listen to the sound and tone of the words. The second time, listen for meaning. Do not look at the reading. Try to follow the ideas by listening only.

As you listen the second time, the speaker will stop occasionally and make statements about the reading. Decide if the statements are true or false. Fill in the space of the circled T or F according to what you hear and remember from the reading.

1. (T) (F)   5. (T) (F)

2. (T) (F)   6. (T) (F)

3. (T) (F)   7. (T) (F)

4. (T) (F)   8. (T) (F)

≫ Writing and Discussion Questions

Work with a partner or group to answer these questions.

1. Discuss advantages and disadvantages of wind power. Are you for or against this form of electricity? Why?

 2. Use the Internet to learn about two forms of energy listed below. Write several sentences about each form that you choose. Include a definition, examples, advantages, and disadvantages. Share the information that you learn with the class.

natural gas	coal	nuclear energy	solar power
hydroelectric energy	geothermal energy	hydrogen fuel	tidal power

3. You are on the advising council of a small country. Your president is deciding the best way to make energy for your country. The president asks the members of the council to make an energy plan. Discuss the problem as a group and explain your plan.

⟫ Crossword Puzzle

Complete the puzzle with words from the reading.

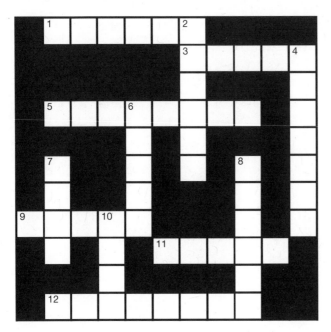

Across

1 The _____ of a wind turbine spin in the wind.

3 Nuclear power plants create _____ wastes.

5 One _____ of wind power is that wind turbines are expensive.

9 Farmers can still raise _____ on land that is used as a wind farm.

11 Soft breezes help us fly _____ in the spring.

12 _____ are destructive wind storms.

Down

2 At sea, the wind is usually strong and _____.

4 The _____ were the first people to use windmills.

6 The sound of a wind turbine is a little like _____ at the beach.

7 A group of wind turbines is called a wind _____.

8 Turbines are placed on top of steel _____.

10 The people of the Netherlands used windmills to _____ seawater.

Yao Ming

Fig. 7.1 Yao Ming.

Before You Read

❯ Warm-Up Questions

Discuss these questions in pairs or groups. Share your ideas with the class.

1. Do you enjoy watching or playing basketball? Why or why not?

2. Have you ever heard of the Chinese basketball player Yao Ming? If so, what do you know about him?

≫ Vocabulary Preview

These statements come from the reading "Yao Ming." Read each statement and then answer the questions. Check your answers before you begin the reading.

Why is there a sudden interest in U.S. basketball?

1. A *sudden* interest . . .

   (A) develops quickly.
   (B) is very strong.
   (C) is hard to explain.

His coaches often tell him to play more aggressively .

2. To play *aggressively* is to play . . .

   (A) intelligently.
   (B) carefully.
   (C) forcefully.

Some standard NBA tactics are considered rude in China.

3. *Standard* means . . .

   (A) modern.
   (B) usual.
   (C) special.

4. *Rude* means . . .

   (A) unpopular.
   (B) friendly.
   (C) impolite.

But Yao is getting used to the U.S. style of playing.

5. *Getting used to* means . . .

   (A) becoming familiar with.
   (B) not being interested in.
   (C) trying to remember.

"He gets attention, obviously , for the way he plays, but people also really like him and his personality."

6. A phrase that means the same thing as *obviously* is . . .

(A) not at all.
(B) in some ways.
(C) of course.

Although he is successful, he is humble .

7. A *humble* person . . .

(A) lives a comfortable life.
(B) does not act as if he is important.
(C) has many problems in his life.

Many U.S. athletes endorse products, and Yao is doing this too.

8. To *endorse* a product is to . . . a product.

(A) say good things about
(B) buy
(C) learn about

He has hired a group of experts called "Team Yao" to find the best opportunities to market products in both the United States and China.

9. *Opportunities* are . . .

(A) locations.
(B) chances to do something.
(C) methods.

Now he speaks mainly through his interpreter , Collin Pine.

10. An *interpreter* is someone who . . .

(A) is as close as a family member.
(B) manages the career of another person.
(C) translates from one language into another.

While You Read

Here are eight points that are discussed in the reading. There is one point for each paragraph. While you read, put the points in order from 1 to 8.

_____ Yao endorses products
_____ A short description of Yao Ming
_____ Yao's popularity and lifestyle in the United States
_____ Yao's English abilities
_____ Yao learns to play U.S. style basketball
_____ China's new interest in U.S. basketball
_____ The internationalization of the NBA
_____ Yao's quick improvement as an NBA basketball player

YAO MING

1   China loves basketball. Chinese fans enjoy watching their favorite teams, such as the Shanghai Sharks and the Beijing Ducks. They also love their national team, which plays in the Asia Games and the Olympics. But more and more fans watch NBA[1] basketball games from the United States. In fact, since 2002, fifteen million Chinese fans have been staying home from work or school to watch one NBA team play. Why is there a sudden interest in U.S. basketball?

2   The answer is Yao Ming. Yao is a young basketball player from Shanghai. He has short hair and a warm smile, and he is very tall (2.3 meters). The son of two professional basketball players, Yao was a star player for the Shanghai Sharks. In 2002, he joined the Houston Rockets, an NBA team in the United States.

3   Yao arrived in Houston in October, at the beginning of the NBA season.[2] He did not have much time to practice with his new team. In his first few games, he was not very good. He scored only about four points a game. However, that changed quickly. In November, he scored twenty points against the Los Angeles Lakers. Then he scored thirty. Soon, he was one of the NBA's best shooters.[3] He hit[4] thirty out of thirty-four shots in three games. He can also pass[5] and rebound[6] well.

4   These days, Yao is learning to play basketball in a different culture. His coaches often tell him to play more aggressively. In China, the success of the team is more important than the success of individuals. In the United States, the opposite is often true. Some standard NBA tactics are considered rude in China. But Yao is getting used to the U.S. style of playing. Yao's coaches also tell him to eat more so that he will be heavier and stronger. His favorite food is his mother's soup, which does not have many calories. Luckily, Yao now also likes to eat pizza.

5   Yao has many fans in the United States. "Everybody loves him," says Rockets' manager Carroll Dawson. "He gets attention, obviously, for the way he plays, but people also really like him and his personality." Although he is successful, he is humble. He lives with his parents and he enjoys watching action movies and playing computer games.

6   Because he is a popular player, Yao can make a lot of money. Many U.S. athletes endorse products, and Yao is doing this too. He has hired a group of experts called "Team Yao" to find the best opportunities to market products in both the United States

Fig. 7.2 Yao Ming shooting a basket.

and China. However, Yao will not endorse products he doesn't use or like.

Yao may become even more popular as he learns more English. Now he speaks mainly through his interpreter, Colin Pine. "I'm still a student," Yao says. However, his teammates say that he understands almost everything they say to him and that he often uses slang.

Yao was not the first international player on a U.S. team. The NBA began looking for international players in the 1980s. Today there are sixty-five international players from thirty-five countries. "Basketball is an international language," says NBA commissioner David Stern. Yao Ming speaks that language as well as anyone.

Notes

1. *NBA* stands for National Basketball Association. This is the professional basketball organization in the United States.

2. The *NBA season* is the time of year when NBA teams play. The season runs from October to June.

3. A good *shooter* is a player who scores a lot of points by shooting baskets (throwing the ball through the basket).

4. To *hit a shot* is to score points by throwing the ball through the basket.

5. To *pass* is to throw the ball to another player on your own team.

6. To *rebound* is to get the ball after another player shoots at the basket but misses.

After You Read

❯ Understanding the Reading

Answer these multiple-choice questions to see how well you understood the reading.

1. Which of these teams did Yao first play for?

   (A) The Beijing Ducks
   (B) The Houston Rockets
   (C) The Shanghai Sharks

2. What jobs did Yao's parents have?

   (A) Basketball players
   (B) Interpreters
   (C) Basketball coaches

3. How many points did Yao score in his first NBA game?

   (A) 4
   (B) 20
   (C) 30

4. How does the reading describe U.S. basketball generally?

   (A) The success of the team is always more important than the success of a single player.
   (B) A player's success may be more important than the success of the team.
   (C) The players are never rude.

5. What food do Yao's coaches probably encourage him to eat?

   (A) Soup
   (B) Pizza
   (C) Rice

6. The reading does NOT say that Yao likes . . .

   (A) watching action movies.
   (B) driving fast automobiles.
   (C) playing computer games.

7. What is "Team Yao"?

    (A) A group of marketing experts
    (B) A Chinese basketball team
    (C) An international basketball team

8. How many NBA players are from countries other than the United States?

    (A) 15
    (B) 35
    (C) 65

❯ Vocabulary Building

Fill in the blanks in the sentences below with one of these words or phrases from the reading.

fan	calories	aggressively	sudden
personality	endorse	opportunities	get used to

1. Anthony is from Australia, so he is accustomed to driving on the left side of the road. It took him some time to _____ driving on the right side on the road in the United States.

2. Always look for _____ to practice your English!

3. Betsy has a warm and friendly _____.

4. Jaime did not find _____ success as an actor. He struggled for many years before he became a star.

5. Many sports stars _____ products such as athletic shoes.

6. Amy drives so fast and _____ that I am surprised she has never gotten a ticket or had an accident.

7. The word _____ comes from the word "fanatic." This person is extremely interested in something, such as a sports team, an entertainer, or an activity.

8. One piece of chocolate cake has more _____ than twenty pieces of celery.

Reading Skill: Scanning 1

Scanning is another method for finding information quickly. In Unit 4, you practiced *skimming*. When you skim, you look for the main ideas of a reading. When you scan, you look for specific facts. Scanning helps you in many situations: researching a report, searching a Web site, looking at a bus schedule, or answering questions on tests such as the TOEFL® or TOEIC®.

Use these tools for scanning:

1. Decide the specific kind of information you are looking for. For example, location (*where*), time (*when*), method (*how*), number (*how many*), and reason (*why*).

2. Think of key terms connected to the information.

3. Read the text quickly looking for this information or these terms.

Exercise: The following questions ask about different kinds of facts in the reading. Underline some key terms in each question. Then scan the reading to locate the terms. Write the number of the paragraph (1–8) in the blank below.

One question is not answered in the reading. Put an **X** by this question.

The first one is done as an example.

1. __4__ What do Chinese players think about standard NBA tactics?

2. _____ Why did Yao Ming have problems in the first NBA game he played?

3. _____ Where does "Team Yao" plan to market products?

4. _____ What is Yao Ming's favorite food?

5. _____ Why do Yao Ming's coaches tell him to eat more?

6. _____ How tall is Yao Ming?

7. _____ Who does Yao Ming live with?

8. _____ How many Chinese fans watch one NBA team every time it plays?

9. _____ Who was the first international player on an NBA team?

10. _____ How many countries today have players in the NBA?

❯ Focus on Listening

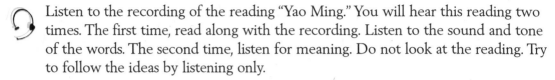

Listen to the recording of the reading "Yao Ming." You will hear this reading two times. The first time, read along with the recording. Listen to the sound and tone of the words. The second time, listen for meaning. Do not look at the reading. Try to follow the ideas by listening only.

As you listen the second time, the speaker will stop occasionally and make statements about the reading. Decide if the statements are true or false. Fill in the space of the circled T or F according to what you hear and remember from the reading.

1. ⓣ Ⓕ   5. ⓣ Ⓕ

2. ⓣ Ⓕ   6. ⓣ Ⓕ

3. ⓣ Ⓕ   7. ⓣ Ⓕ

4. ⓣ Ⓕ   8. ⓣ Ⓕ

❯ Writing and Discussion Questions

Work with a partner or group to answer these questions.

1. Do you ever buy a product because an athlete or an entertainer that you like endorses it? Why or why not?

2. Professional athletes can make a lot of money. Is it fair for them to make much more money than, for example, nurses or teachers? Why or why not?

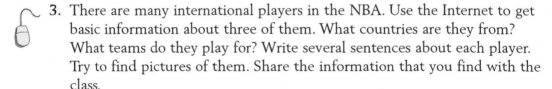

3. There are many international players in the NBA. Use the Internet to get basic information about three of them. What countries are they from? What teams do they play for? Write several sentences about each player. Try to find pictures of them. Share the information that you find with the class.

❯ Crossword Puzzle

Complete the puzzle with words from the reading.

Across

2 Yao now enjoys eating _____.

3 Yao's mother's _____ does not have many calories.

5 Yao does not _____ products that he doesn't like or use.

6 Yao is popular with _____ in both China and the United States.

8 The _____ first began looking for international players in the 1980s.

10 In his first season, Yao scored twenty points against the Los Angeles _____.

11 After leaving China, Yao began to play for the Houston _____.

Down

1 There has been a _____ growth in interest in the NBA in China.

2 People like Yao for his ability to play and for his _____.

4 Some NBA _____ would be considered rude in China.

7 Yao first played for the Shanghai _____.

9 Yao has a _____ smile.

Esperanto as a Second Language

Fig. 8.1 L. L. Zamenhof, the inventor of Esperanto.

Before You Read

» Warm-Up Questions

Discuss these questions in pairs or groups. Share your ideas with the class.

1. This reading is about Esperanto, an "artificial" language. What is an artificial language? What are some reasons for creating an artificial language?

2. If everyone speaks the same second language, will it help the world? Why or why not?

❯ Vocabulary Preview

These statements come from the reading "Esperanto as a Second Language."
Read each statement and then answer the questions. Check your answers before
you begin the reading.

And people all over the world can speak as equals —not in your language, not in
theirs, but in a universal language.

1. In this sentence, *equals* refers to . . .

   (A) two languages that are equally difficult.
   (B) equal amounts of time.
   (C) people who are at the same level.

2. A *universal* language is . . .

   (A) spoken by almost everyone.
   (B) easy to learn.
   (C) not modern.

Speakers of different languages did not understand each other and there was often
conflict between the various groups.

3. *Conflict* is . . .

   (A) understanding.
   (B) fighting.
   (C) discussion.

From a young age, he wanted to overcome language problems by introducing an
international language.

4. To *overcome* problems is to . . . them.

   (A) study
   (B) solve
   (C) find

Then Zamenhoff studied the artificial language *Volapük*, which was created in 1879
by Johann Schleyer, but he decided that this language was not easy enough either.
Therefore, he invented Esperanto.

5. Circle the word that is close in meaning to *invented*.

Because Esperanto is a planned language, it is logical and simple.

6. *Logical* means . . .

   (A) interesting.
   (B) limited.
   (C) reasonable.

Word order in Esperanto is very flexible .

7. A *flexible* word order . . .

   (A) is very unusual.
   (B) is very difficult to learn.
   (C) does not follow strict rules.

Compared to natural languages, there are few idioms or slang words .

8. *Slang words* are examples of . . .

   (A) language mistakes.
   (B) informal language.
   (C) impolite language.

However, unlike English, Esperanto is politically neutral .

9. *Neutral* means . . .

   (A) not on one side or the other.
   (B) unimportant.
   (C) active.

The grammar of English is simple, but there are many exceptions to the rules.

10. An *exception* is . . .

   (A) something that breaks a rule.
   (B) an example of a rule.
   (C) a simple type of grammar.

While You Read

Here are six points that are discussed in the reading. There is one point for each paragraph. While you read, put the points in order from 1 to 6.

_____ Dr. Zamenhof's dream
_____ The slow growth of Esperanto
_____ The early history of Esperanto
_____ A description of Esperanto
_____ The reason Dr. Zamenhof invented Esperanto
_____ The problems of English as an international language

ESPERANTO AS A SECOND LANGUAGE

1   Imagine this: Everyone learns the same second language in school. Everywhere you go, people can speak this language. And people all over the world speak as equals—not in your language, not in theirs, but in a universal language. This was the dream of Dr. L. L. Zamenhof, the inventor of Esperanto.

2   L. L. Zamenhof was born in 1859 in Bialystok, Poland (then part of Russia). The people of Bialystok spoke Polish, Yiddish, German, Russian, and Lithuanian. Speakers of the various languages did not understand each other and there was often conflict among the various groups. Zamenhof believed that the problems in his city and all over the world came from differences in language. From a young age, he wanted to overcome language problems by introducing an international language. At first he planned to bring back Latin.[1] However, he studied Latin at school and decided it was too difficult. Then Zamenhof studied the artificial language Volapük, which was created in 1879 by Johann Schleyer, but he decided that this

language was not easy enough either. Therefore, he invented Esperanto.

3   After years of work, Zamenhof finished a book about his language in 1887. Zamenhof used the pen name[2] Doktoro Esperanto, which means "a person who hopes." At first, his language was called "lingvo internacia de la Doktoro Esperanto."[3] This name was too long and soon people called the language Esperanto. In a few years, hundreds of thousands of people learned Zamenhof's language. "Esperantists" from all over the world shared Zamenhof's dream. They started the Universal Esperanto Association and had their first international meeting in France in 1905.

4   Because Esperanto is a planned language, it is logical and simple. It can be learned in one quarter the time of a typical natural language. Spelling and pronunciation are easy. Each letter has only one sound. The grammar is simple, too. There are sixteen basic rules, with no exceptions. Word order in Esperanto is very flexible. For example, you can correctly say *blau domo* (blue house) or *domo blau* (house blue). Compared to natural languages, there are few idioms or slang words. About 75% of the vocabulary of Esperanto comes from Romance languages such as French and Spanish. About 20% comes from German and English. The rest comes from Slavic languages such as Russian and Polish.

5   Some people say that an international language is unnecessary. They say that today, English is the international

language. It is true that English is a second language for many people. However, unlike English, Esperanto is politically neutral. Besides, pronunciation and spelling in English are difficult. The grammar of English is simple, but there are many exceptions to the rules.

6   Today, there are books, magazines, websites, and radio broadcasts in Esperanto. About two million people speak Esperanto. However, the number of new Esperanto speakers is growing very slowly. Could Esperanto really change the world? No one knows. Zamenhof's idea—that people everywhere learn Esperanto as a second language—is still just a dream.

Notes

1. *Latin* was the language of the Roman Empire. It was also used as an international language in the past.

2. A *pen name* is a name that a person uses when he or she writes a book. It is not the person's real name.

3. In Esperanto, this phrase means "the international language of Dr. Esperanto."

After You Read

≫ Understanding the Reading

Answer these multiple-choice questions to see how well you understood the reading.

1. Which of these languages did Zamenhof first plan to use as an international language?

   (A) Esperanto
   (B) Volapük
   (C) Latin

2. L. L. Zamenhof introduced Esperanto to the world in . . .

(A) 1879.
(B) 1887.
(C) 1905.

3. Why was the original name of Esperanto changed?

(A) The original name made many people angry.
(B) The original name was too long.
(C) The original name was difficult to pronounce.

4. If it takes a person two years to learn a typical natural language, how long will it probably take that person to learn Esperanto?

(A) Six months
(B) One year
(C) Eight years

5. What are the phrases *blau domo* and *domo blau* given as examples of?

(A) Esperanto words that come from Romance languages
(B) The simple spelling and pronunciation of Esperanto
(C) The flexible word order of Esperanto

6. About how much of Esperanto vocabulary comes from Slavic languages?

(A) 5%
(B) 20%
(C) 75%

7. What does the author say about the grammar of English?

(A) It is simple compared to the grammar of Esperanto.
(B) It is not difficult but it has many exceptions.
(C) It is harder than the grammar of most natural languages.

8. What does the author say about the use of Esperanto today?

(A) It is growing quickly.
(B) It is decreasing slowly.
(C) It is growing slowly.

➤ Vocabulary Building

Fill in the blanks in the sentences below with one of these words from the reading.

equals	universal	conflict	artificial
logical	exceptions	flexible	neutral

1. If a lake is not made by nature, it is an _____ lake.

2. In a formal debate, your arguments should be _____, not emotional.

3. Jan's work schedule is _____; she can work in the afternoon or in the morning.

4. Prepositions are difficult to use in English because there are so many _____ to the rules.

5. During World War II, Sweden was a _____ nation. It did not fight on either side.

6. Now that my brothers and I are adults, our parents treat us as _____.

7. All people in the world need food and shelter. These are _____ needs.

8. The United Nations was founded to help reduce the amount of _____ between countries.

Reading Skill: Skimming 2

In Unit 4, you practiced skimming by finding summary sentences. Another way is the whole text method. In this method, you move your eyes quickly over the entire text. This method is helpful when the main idea is not directly stated, or when topic sentences and thesis statements are difficult to find.

Remember:

- Read quickly, about three to four times as fast as your normal speed.

- Don't try to understand more than about 50% of the material.

- Don't worry about vocabulary that you don't understand.

- Don't pay attention to details.

Exercise: Skim the reading below in two minutes. Then answer the question that follows. Mark your beginning time and ending time.

Beginning time: _____

After World War I, many nations formed the League of Nations. The League's goal was to prevent another war. Because the League was an important international organization, Esperantists wanted it to use Esperanto as its official language. The Esperantists believed that if the League spoke Esperanto, all nations would learn Esperanto, and soon everyone in the world would speak the same second language. In 1921, the League chose a committee of ten members to discuss the issue and vote on it. The final vote was nine to one in favor of using Esperanto. One member, Gabriel Hanotaux, voted no. At the time, French was the leading international language. Hanotaux believed that Esperanto would replace French. The vote had to be unanimous, and, therefore, the proposal was not accepted.

After World War II, a similar situation happened with the United Nations (U.N.). More than 500,000 people and 500 organizations wanted the U.N. to use Esperanto as its main language. They signed a petition and sent it to the U.N. At a special meeting in Uruguay, some linguists spoke in favor of this idea, and some spoke against it. The final vote was six to one against Esperanto. The U.N. later decided to use six major languages—English, French, Russian, Spanish, Arabic, and Chinese—as the official languages of the United Nations.

Ending time:____

What is the main idea of this reading?

    (A) The League of Nations was not as strong as the United Nations.
    (B) Both the League of Nations and the United Nations decided not to use Esperanto.
    (C) Six major languages were chosen as the official languages of the United Nations.
    (D) Esperanto was accepted by the League of Nations but not by the United Nations.

➤ Focus on Listening

Listen to the recording of the reading "Esperanto as a Second Language." You will hear this reading two times. The first time, read along with the recording. Listen to the sound and tone of the words. The second time, listen for meaning. Do not look at the reading. Try to follow the ideas by listening only.

As you listen the second time, the speaker will stop occasionally and make statements about the reading. Decide if the statements are true or false. Fill in the space of the circled T or F according to what you hear and remember from the reading.

1. Ⓣ Ⓕ   5. Ⓣ Ⓕ

2. Ⓣ Ⓕ   6. Ⓣ Ⓕ

3. Ⓣ Ⓕ   7. Ⓣ Ⓕ

4. Ⓣ Ⓕ   8. Ⓣ Ⓕ

➤ Writing and Discussion Questions

Work with a partner or group to answer these questions.

1. Do you think Esperanto will ever become a universal second language? Why or why not?

2. Here is a paragraph in Esperanto. As a group, try to translate the paragraph into English. If there are parts of the paragraph that you can't translate, guess. (There is a translation in the answer key.)

   Inteligenta persono lernas la lingvon Esperanto rapide kaj facile. Esperanto estas la moderna lingvo por la tuta mondo. Simpla, fleksebla, belsona, ĝi estas la praktika solvo de la problemo de universala interkompreno. Esperanto meritas vian seriozan konsideron. Lernu la internacian lingvon Esperanto!

3. In addition to Esperanto, there are many other artificial languages. Using the Internet, get some information about two of the artificial languages listed below. Find out when they were invented, who invented them, why they were invented, and other basic facts. Write several sentences about each of the two languages that you choose. Share the information that you learn with the class.

Solresol	Ido	Lingvo Kosmopolita	Interlingua
Novial	Neo	Quenya	Occidental
Pidgin English	Klingon	Loglan and Lojban	Monario
Pasigraphy	Volapük	Interglossa and Glossa	Idiom Neutral

» Crossword Puzzle

Complete the puzzle with words from the reading.

Across

1   Word order in Esperanto is very
    _____.

5   Esperanto is politically _____.

7   The word *Esperanto* means "one
    who _____."

9   There are few idioms or _____
    words in Esperanto.

10 The artificial language _____
    was created in 1879.

11 Some words in Esperanto come
    from _____ languages such as
    Russian or Polish.

Down

2   Zamenhof was born in the town
    of _____.

3   "Doctoro Esperanto" was
    Zamenhof's _____ name.

4   Many words in Esperanto come
    from _____ languages such as
    French or Spanish.

6   Esperanto is _____ and simple
    because it is a planned language.

8   Esperantists can speak to one
    another as _____.

Mystery on Mount Everest

Fig. 9.1 George Mallory, mountain climber.

Before You Read

❯ Warm-Up Questions

Discuss these questions in pairs or groups. Share your ideas with the class.

1. Look at the photograph. Where do you think this photograph was taken? When do you think it was taken?

2. What do you know about Sir Edmund Hillary and Tenzing Norgay?

❯ Vocabulary Preview

These statements come from the reading "Mystery on Mount Everest." Read each statement and then answer the questions. Check your answers before you begin the reading.

Sir Edmund Hillary and Tenzing Norgay climbed to the   peak   of Mount Everest in 1953. For fifty years, history books have said that Hillary and Norgay were the first to get to the top, but history might be wrong.

1. Circle a word in the sentences above that has the same meaning as *peak*.

On the next trip, in 1922, he attempted to climb to the top of Everest but a huge avalanche   killed seven Tibetan guides and almost killed Mallory.

2. What happens during an *avalanche*?

(A) Winds blow very hard.
(B) Snow falls from a mountain above.
(C) The earth shakes.

Irvine was an engineering student. He was not an   experienced   climber, but he was an expert on oxygen equipment.

3. Irvine was not an *experienced* climber. This means that he . . .

(A) was not afraid of any dangers.
(B) did not cooperate well with other climbers.
(C) had not climbed many mountains in the past.

Mallory and Irvine were   behind schedule   but were "going strong" 250 meters below the top.

4. *Behind schedule* means that Mallory and Irvine . . .

(A) did not have a schedule.
(B) were not climbing as fast as they wanted to.
(C) were moving very quickly.

It is hard to believe that Mallory and Irvine climbed this steep rock wall with their poor equipment.

5. Which picture shows a *steep* rock wall?

(A)

(B)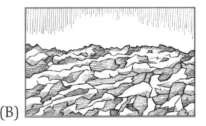

(C)

However, many others think the challenge was almost impossible.

6. A *challenge* is something that is . . . to do.

(A) difficult
(B) impossible
(C) easy

The camera may be the key to the mystery.

7. This sentence means that the camera may . . . the mystery.

(A) cause
(B) solve
(C) deepen

Photography experts say that the film in Mallory's camera can still be developed if the camera was never opened.

8. In this sentence, *developed* means that . . .

(A) pictures can be made from the film.
(B) the film can be located.
(C) the film can be used again.

Mallory may have reached the summit .

9. A *summit* is the . . . a mountain.

(A) most dangerous place on
(B) foot of
(C) top of

"Although he is a heroic figure, he didn't quite complete the job." . . . but he was still a brave explorer of the world's highest and most dangerous mountain.

10. Circle the word that is close in meaning to *heroic*.

While You Read

Here are eight points that are discussed in the reading. There is one point for each paragraph. While you read, put the points in order from 1 to 8.

_____ Mallory and Irvine leave camp on June 6
_____ The camera, key to the mystery
_____ Mallory's equipment and then Mallory's body are found
_____ Mallory's first two trips to Everest
_____ The mystery: Did Malloy and Irvine reach the top?
_____ Hillary's opinion of Mallory's climb
_____ The last sight of Mallory and Irvine
_____ Who the history books say first climbed Everest

MYSTERY ON MOUNT EVEREST

Fig. 9.2 Mount Everest.

Sir Edmund Hillary and Tenzing Norgay climbed to the peak of Mount Everest[1] in 1953. For fifty years, history books have said that Hillary and Norgay were the first to get to the top, but history might be wrong.

George Mallory was a British schoolteacher and an excellent climber. Mallory went to Mount Everest several times in the early 1920s. On the first trip in 1921, he helped to map Mount Everest. On the next trip, in 1922, he attempted to climb to the top of Everest but a huge avalanche killed seven Tibetan guides and almost killed Mallory. Although it was dangerous, Mallory wanted to try again. During a lecture tour of the United States in 1923, a reporter asked the explorer, "Why do you want to climb Everest?" Mallory's answer became famous: "Because it's there."

In 1924, Mallory returned to Mount Everest. This time, he was going to try very hard to get to the top. His team set up camps on the mountainside. The highest was Camp 6, at 8,140 meters. On the morning of June 6, he and a young climber named Sandy Irvine left camp. Irvine was an engineering student. He was not an experienced climber, but he was an expert on oxygen equipment.[2] When they left camp, Mallory borrowed a camera from another team member.

4   At 12:50 that afternoon, the team's movie maker, Noel Odell, saw Mallory and Irvine far above him. Mallory and Irvine were behind schedule but were "going strong" 250 meters below the top. Then, a cloud covered the peak. No one ever saw Mallory and Irvine alive again.

5   A few years later, other mountain climbers found some of Mallory's equipment. In 1933, British climbers found Irvine's ice axe.[3] In 1975, a Chinese climber said that he saw a body in old climbing clothes. Then, in 1999, a U.S. team that was looking for Mallory and Irvine found a frozen body at 8,400 meters. DNA testing showed that it was George Mallory. The team did not find Irvine or the camera.

6   The mystery is *when* Mallory died. Did he die climbing to the peak or coming down from the peak? The climber's clothing, boots, ropes, tools, and oxygen equipment were not very good compared to modern equipment. There is an especially difficult wall of rock, called the Second Step, just below the peak. It is hard to believe that Mallory and Irvine climbed this steep rock wall with their poor equipment. Some climbing experts believe Mallory and Irvine probably were successful. However, many others think the challenge was almost impossible. No one knows for sure.

7   **Fig. 9.3** Some of Mallory's personal property recovered from the mountain.

The camera may be the key to the mystery. When Hillary and

Norgay climbed to the top, they immediately took pictures of each other. Perhaps Mallory and Irvine did the same. Photography experts say that the film in Mallory's camera can still be developed if the camera was never opened.

8   Sir Edmund Hillary said that it is not important who was first to the top. Hillary said, "Who knows? Mallory may have reached the summit. Probably he didn't. But he certainly did not reach the bottom. . . . Although he is a heroic figure, he didn't quite complete the job." It is true that Mallory probably did not finish the climb, but he was still a brave explorer of the world's highest and most dangerous mountain.

Notes

1. *Mount Everest*, which is 8,840 meters high, is the highest mountain in the world. It is in the Himalayan Mountains between Nepal and Tibet.

2. On high mountains such as Mount Everest, climbers need to carry their own *oxygen equipment* because there is not enough oxygen to breathe at that altitude.

3. An *ice axe* is a tool for climbing mountains.

After You Read

» Understanding the Reading

Answer these multiple-choice questions to see how well you understood the reading.

1. How many years passed between Mallory's last attempt to climb Everest and Hillary's successful climb?

    (A) About 20
    (B) About 30
    (C) About 40

2. On which of Mallory's trips to Mount Everest were seven guides killed?

(A) His first
(B) His second
(C) His third

3. Mallory went to the United States to . . .

(A) climb mountains.
(B) make maps.
(C) give lectures.

4. Why was Irvine probably chosen to climb with Mallory?

(A) He knew a lot about oxygen equipment.
(B) He was a well trained and experienced mountain climber.
(C) He knew a lot about cameras and movie-making.

5. When was Mallory's body actually found?

(A) 1933
(B) 1975
(C) 1999

6. In this reading, the phrase "Second Step" refers to . . .

(A) Mallory's second trip to Mount Everest.
(B) a difficult part of the mountain to climb.
(C) Hillary and Norgay's climb in 1953.

7. Which of these statements would Sir Edmund Hillary agree with?

(A) "Now we know that Mallory was the first person to climb Everest."
(B) "Mallory is not really a brave, heroic climber."
(C) "Mallory may have reached the top, but he didn't return."

8. The title of this reading is "Mystery on Mount Everest." What is the mystery that the title refers to?

(A) Were Mallory and Irvine the first to climb Everest?
(B) What happened to Mallory's body?
(C) Were Mallory and Irvine murdered?

❯ Vocabulary Building

Fill in the blanks in the sentences below with one of these words from the reading.

steep   developed   summit   challenge
borrowed   experienced   heroic   avalanche

1. When I was in high school, I had a darkroom at home and I
   _____ my own black-and-white photographs.

2. Mr. Jackson jumped into the freezing river and saved a child who was
   drowning. He received a gold medal for his _____ act.

3. I tried to ride my bicycle up the hill, but the hill was too

   _____.

4. The highest point on the continent of Africa is the _____ of
   Mount Kilimanjaro in Tanzania.

5. A: Are you taking Professor Yang's calculus class? It's really hard.

   B: That's all right, I like a _____.

6. I read in the newspaper that a small village in the Swiss Alps was almost
   buried by an _____.

7. A: I applied for a job as a manager of a bookstore.

   B: Did you get the job?

   A: No, I've never worked in a bookstore before, and they wanted
      someone who was _____.

8. A: Nice car! Is it yours?

   B: No, I _____ it from my brother.

Reading Skill: Understanding Word Families

A good way to learn vocabulary is to keep a "word family" notebook. This way, you study words with similar meaning at the same time. For most people, it is easier to learn a group of related words than a list of unrelated words.

Here is how it works. When you find an unfamiliar word, write it down in your notebook and draw a circle around it. Next, look for synonyms or similar words. You may find synonyms in the reading, a general dictionary, a thesaurus (a synonym and antonym dictionary), or the thesaurus function that comes with most word processing programs such as MS Word® and WordPerfect®.

For example, suppose you need to learn the word *huge* in line 13.

Example

Using a dictionary or a computer, you may find some other words with meanings similar to huge.

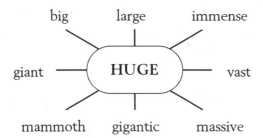

big large immense

giant — HUGE — vast

mammoth gigantic massive

Exercise:

Part 1: Make a word-family diagram for each of these words from the reading. Find at least three synonyms for each term. Use the example as a model.

EXCELLENT

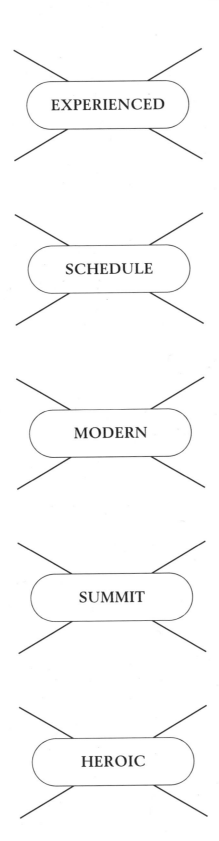

EXPERIENCED

SCHEDULE

MODERN

SUMMIT

HEROIC

Part 2: Look at the term in **bold**. Then circle the word on the line next to it that is NOT part of the same word family.

1. **excellent**	wonderful	outstanding	available	terrific
2. **experienced**	trained	veteran	humble	skillful
3. **schedule**	statue	plan	program	timetable
4. **modern**	up-to-date	current	new	useful
5. **summit**	peak	top	base	high point
6. **heroic**	brave	careful	courageous	daring

❱ Focus on Listening

Listen to the recording of the reading "Mystery on Mount Everest." You will hear this reading two times. The first time, read along with the recording. Listen to the sound and tone of the words. The second time, listen for meaning. Do not look at the reading. Try to follow the ideas by listening only.

As you listen the second time, the speaker will stop occasionally and make statements about the reading. Decide if the statements are true or false. Fill in the space of the circled T or F according to what you hear and remember from the reading.

1. T F   5. T F
2. T F   6. T F
3. T F   7. T F
4. T F   8. T F

❱ Writing and Discussion Questions

Work with a partner or group to answer these questions.

1. Do you think Mallory reached the top of Everest? Why or why not? Use information from the reading to explain your opinion.

2. Thomas Mallory said that he climbed Mount Everest "because it's there." Why do you think people climb mountains?

3. These are the names of some other mountains that challenge climbers. Using the Internet, get some basic information about three of them. If possible, include these facts: continent, country, height, who first climbed them, and when.

Popocatepetl	Fuji	Mount Erebus	Mount Kosciusko
El Capitan	El Torre	Mont Blanc	Denali (Mount McKinley)
Aconcagua	Kilimanjaro	Nanga Parbat	Aoraki (Mount Cook)

Write several sentences about each of the mountains that you choose. Share the information that you find with the class.

❯ Crossword Puzzle

Complete the puzzle with words from the reading.

Across

1 Mount Everest's _____ is 8,849 meters high.

4 In 1922, seven guides died in a huge _____.

7 Tenzing _____ and Sir Edmund Hillary climbed Mount Everest in 1953.

8 The Second Step is a _____ rock wall.

9 Mallory was a schoolteacher and an _____ climber.

10 Irvine was an expert on _____ equipment.

Down

2 In 1999, a team of American climbers found the body of _____.

3 Experts believe the film can still be _____.

5 Mount _____ is the world's highest mountain.

6 The _____ is that no one knows if Mallory and Irvine reached the summit.

Danger: Asteroids Ahead?

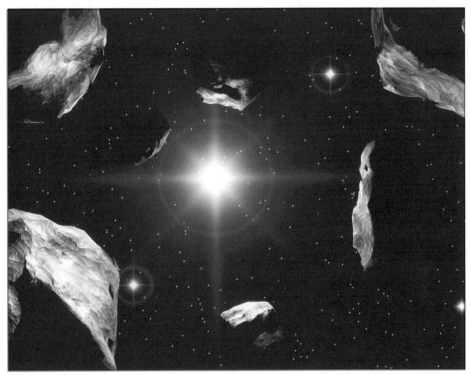

Fig. 10.1 Asteroids.

Before You Read

❯ Warm-Up Questions

Discuss these questions in pairs or groups. Share your ideas with the class.

1. What are asteroids? Look at the picture and try to describe them.

2. What danger do you think people could face from asteroids?

≫ Vocabulary Preview

These statements come from the reading "Danger: Asteroids Ahead?" Read each statement and then answer the questions. Check your answers before you begin the reading.

Scientists did not see the asteroid until three days after it passed. To astronomers, this was a near miss .

1. A *near miss* means that an object . . .

   (A) almost hits something, but doesn't.
   (B) hits something, but not hard.
   (C) doesn't come close to another object.

Scientists believe that dinosaurs died out because an immense asteroid, perhaps 10 kilometers in diameter, ran into the Earth.

2. An *immense* asteroid is a . . . one.

   (A) speeding
   (B) dangerous
   (C) large

When the asteroid hit the Earth, it threw ash and dust into the air.

3. *Ash* is . . .

   (A) a cloud of poisonous gas.
   (B) the powder that is left after something burns.
   (C) a large wave of water.

4. *Dust* is . . .

   (A) tiny pieces of rock and earth.
   (B) flame and smoke.
   (C) light and noise.

It knocked down over 2,000 square kilometers of forest .

5. In a *forest* there are many . . .

   (A) buildings.
   (B) trees.
   (C) mountains.

An asteroid 10 kilometers wide—the size of the "dinosaur killer"—might wipe out human civilization. But don't panic !

6. To *panic* means to . . .

   (A) think about something for a long time.
   (B) be afraid.
   (C) make other plans.

Tunguska-size asteroids hit the Earth every 100 to 1,000 years. Asteroids that cause global damage strike the Earth only about every 100,000 years.

7. Circle the word in the sentences above that has the same meaning as *strike*.

First, most asteroids are small and dark. That makes them difficult to spot .

8. To *spot* an asteroid is to . . . it.

   (A) destroy
   (B) travel to
   (C) see

Scientists think it might be possible to send a spacecraft to the asteroid to destroy it or to change its course .

9. The asteroid's *course* is its . . .

   (A) speed.
   (B) direction.
   (C) shape.

They also say that our planet has survived for millions of years without protection from asteroids.

10. If people have *survived*, they have . . .

   (A) been in danger but stayed alive.
   (B) been very worried.
   (C) not understood the danger.

Note: There are a number of phrasal verbs (such as *ran into* and *cut off*) in this reading. These are discussed in the Reading Skill section on page 117. You may want to read this section and do the exercise before reading the passage.

While You Read

Here are seven points that are discussed in the reading. There is one point for each paragraph. While you read, put the points in order from 1 to 7.

_____ An asteroid passes close to Earth
_____ What astronauts can do if an asteroid approaches Earth
_____ The problems of locating asteroids
_____ Two opinions about a program to look for asteroids
_____ A definition of asteroids and near-Earth asteroids
_____ The damage asteroids can cause
_____ Two asteroids that hit the Earth in the past

DANGER: ASTEROIDS AHEAD?

1   Asteroid 2002 MN flew past Earth on June 14, 2002. It passed only 75,000 miles from our planet. This is closer to the Earth than the moon. There was no warning that 2002 MN was coming. Scientists did not see the asteroid until three days after it passed. To astronomers, this was a near miss.

2   The word *asteroid* means "little star." Asteroids are not stars, however; they are actually pieces of rock. Most asteroids are found between the orbits of Jupiter and Mars, but some, called near-Earth asteroids (NEAs), come close to Earth. Of the eight hundred known as NEAs, about six hundred are not dangerous. However, one of the other NEAs might run into the Earth someday.

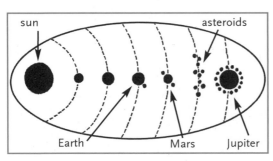

Fig. 10.2 A part of the solar system.

3   It has happened in the past. Scientists believe that dinosaurs died out because an immense asteroid, perhaps 10 kilometers in diameter, ran into the Earth. When the asteroid hit the Earth, it threw ash and dust into the air. The ash and dust cut off the sun's light. Temperatures fell, plants died, and there was not enough food for the dinosaurs. Scientists also believe that an asteroid about the size of 2002 MN (100 meters in diameter) fell near the town of Tunguska in Siberia in 1908. It knocked down over 2,000 square kilometers of forest.

4   How much damage can an asteroid cause? That depends on its size. A Tunguska-size asteroid can destroy an area the size of a city. An asteroid 10 kilometers wide—the size of the "dinosaur killer"—might wipe out human civilization. But don't panic! The chance that an asteroid will hit the Earth is real, but not very high. Tunguska-size asteroids hit the Earth every 100 to 1,000 years. Asteroids that cause global damage strike the Earth only about every 100,000 years.

5   Today, the governments of several countries try to locate NEAs. University and amateur astronomers also watch out for dangerous asteroids. However, there are problems. First, most asteroids are small and dark. That makes them difficult to spot. Second, if an asteroid is coming from the direction of the sun, it cannot be seen because the sun is too bright. Finally, there is no large-scale program in the southern hemisphere to try to find asteroids.

6   If an asteroid is heading for Earth, what can we do? Scientists think it might be possible to send a spacecraft to the

Fig. 10.3 Scene from *Armageddon*.

asteroid to destroy it or to change its course. In the movie *Armageddon* (1998), astronauts use a nuclear bomb to blow up the asteroid. This was exciting to watch, but probably too dangerous to actually do. The explosion might create many smaller asteroids heading for Earth. Instead of using a bomb, astronauts could use rocket engines to push the asteroid out of Earth's path.

7   Some people believe we need a serious program to look for asteroids. This program would probably cost a trillion U.S. dollars ($1,000,000,000,000). People who are in favor of this program think that the danger is more important than the cost. Other people think that this is a waste of money. They say that we should spend the money to solve problems on Earth. They also say that our planet has survived for millions of years without protection from asteroids.

After You Read

❯ Understanding the Reading

Answer these multiple-choice questions to see how well you understood the reading.

1. When did scientists first see the asteroid 2002 MN?

(A) On June 11
(B) On June 14
(C) On June 17

2. Where are most asteroids found?

(A) Close to the sun
(B) Between the Earth and the moon
(C) Between the orbits of Jupiter and Mars

3. About how many dangerous NEAs are there?

(A) 200
(B) 600
(C) 800

4. Which of these asteroids was the biggest?

(A) 2002 MN
(B) The "dinosaur killer"
(C) The Tunguska asteroid

5. Where did the Tunguska asteroid land?

(A) On a city
(B) In a forest
(C) In the ocean

6. How often do Tunguska-size asteroids hit the Earth?

(A) Once every 100 to 1,000 years
(B) Once every 1,000 to 10,000 years
(C) Once every 100,000 years

7. How many reasons are given to explain why it is hard to see asteroids?

(A) One
(B) Three
(C) Five

8. What does the author think we should do if an asteroid is approaching the Earth?

(A) Use a nuclear bomb to break the asteroid into small pieces
(B) Find safe places to hide
(C) Use rocket engines to change the asteroid's direction

» Vocabulary Building

Fill in the blanks in the sentences below with one of these words from the reading.

immense	amateur	panic	civilization
survived	waste	spot	diameter

Fig. 10.4 The *Titanic*.

1. At first, only _____ athletes competed in the Olympics. Today, many professional athletes compete too.

2. Russia is an _____ country. It's so big that there are ten time zones in Russia.

3. A: Oh no! I just realized we have a test in chemistry class this Tuesday!

   B: Don't _____. The test isn't until next Tuesday.

4. The sinking of the *Titanic* was a terrible disaster. There were 2,201 people on the ship. Only 711 of these people _____.

5. Don't run your engine while you are waiting. That's a _____ of gasoline.

6. Both Rome and Greece contributed a lot to European _____.

7. Johann has a long beard and he usually wears a bright red sweater. He is easy to _____ in a crowd.

8. The moon is 3,480 kilometers in _____.

Reading Skill: Understanding Phrasal Verbs

A *phrasal verb* is a verb used together with one or two other words. A phrasal verb does not have the same meaning as a verb when it is used alone. Look at these two sentences:

> *Turn* left at the next traffic light.

> *Turn up* the radio.

In the first sentence, the verb *turn* used alone means "go in another direction." In the second sentence, the phrasal verb *turn up* means "make it louder" or "increase the volume."

You can use the context of sentences to understand phrasal verbs just as you can with any vocabulary. Also, most dictionaries—especially learners' dictionaries—explain the meaning of phrasal verbs.

Exercise 1: Go through the reading and try to find at least five examples of phrasal verbs. Underline them.

Exercise 2: Below are sentences from the reading that use phrasal verbs. Each is followed by an incomplete sentence. Put a checkmark (✓) by the answer that correctly completes the sentence.

However, one of the other NEAs might run into the Earth someday.

1. An NEA might . . . the Earth.

_____(A) hit

_____(B) miss

Scientists believe that dinosaurs died out because an immense asteroid, perhaps 10 kilometers in diameter, ran into the earth.

2. The dinosaurs became . . .

_____(A) weak.

_____(B) extinct.

The ash and dust cut off the sun's light.

3. There was . . . light from the sun.

_____(A) no

_____(B) more

It knocked down over 2,000 square kilometers of forest.

4. The forest was . . .

_____(A) not standing.

_____(B) burning.

How much damage can an asteroid cause? That depends on its size.

5. The size of the asteroid . . . damage.

_____(A) is not related to the

_____(B) controls the amount of

An asteroid 10 kilometers wide—the size of the "dinosaur killer"—can wipe out human civilization.

6. A ten-kilometer asteroid might . . . human civilization.

_____(A) change

_____(B) destroy

University and amateur astronomers also watch out for dangerous asteroids.

7. The astronomers try to . . . dangerous asteroids.

_____(A) spot

_____(B) photograph

If an asteroid is heading for Earth, what can we do?

8. An asteroid that is *heading for* Earth is moving . . . Earth.

_____(A) toward

_____(B) away from

In the movie *Armageddon* (1998), astronauts use a nuclear bomb to blow up the asteroid.

9. The astronauts . . .

_____(A) destroy the asteroid with an explosion.

_____(B) move the asteroid in another direction.

➤ Focus on Listening

Listen to the recording of the reading "Danger: Asteroids Ahead?" You will hear this reading two times. The first time, read along with the recording. Listen to the sound and tone of the words. The second time, listen for meaning. Do not look at the reading. Try to follow the ideas by listening only.

As you listen the second time, the speaker will stop occasionally and make statements about the reading. Decide if the statements are true or false. Fill in the space of the circled T or F according to what you hear and remember from the reading.

1. (T) (F)   5. (T) (F)

2. (T) (F)   6. (T) (F)

3. (T) (F)   7. (T) (F)

4. (T) (F)   8. (T) (F)

❯ Writing and Discussion Questions

Work with a partner or group to answer these questions.

1. In the last paragraph of the reading, the author presents two sides of an argument. What is the argument? Which side of the argument do you agree with? Why?

2. If possible, watch all or part of the movie *Armageddon*. Discuss the movie after you watch it. Do you think it is entertaining? Do you think it is realistic? Why or why not?

 3. 2002 MN is not the only asteroid that has passed close to the Earth. Using the Internet, get some basic information about two other near-earth asteroids. Find out what their names are, when they passed close to the Earth, how close they passed, and other basic facts. Share the information that you find with the class.

➤ Crossword Puzzle

Complete the puzzle with words from the reading.

Across

1 Astronauts might travel on a _____ to an asteroid.

5 When the "dinosaur-killer" hit the Earth, it threw ash and _____ into the air.

6 Asteroid 2002 _____ almost hit the Earth.

8 Most asteroids are found between the _____ of Jupiter and Saturn.

9 Asteroids coming from the direction of the _____ can't be seen.

11 Some people think a program to look for asteroids is a _____ of money.

12 Some people are in _____ of a program to look for asteroids.

13 Small asteroids _____ the Earth more often than large ones.

Down

2 Both professional and _____ astronomers look for asteroids.

3 An asteroid landed in Siberia near the town of _____.

4 An asteroid 10 kilometers in diameter is _____.

5 Scientists think the _____ died out when an asteroid hit the Earth.

7 A very large asteroid could _____ out human civilization.

10 An asteroid found near the Earth is called an _____.

Machu Picchu, City in the Clouds

Fig. 11.1 Machu Picchu.

Before You Read

» Warm-Up Questions

Discuss these questions in pairs or groups. Share your ideas with the class.

1. Have you ever heard of the city of Machu Picchu? If so, what do you know about it?

2. Look at the title of the reading and the photograph of Machu Picchu. What do they tell you about the location of the city?

❯ Vocabulary Preview

These statements come from the reading "Machu Picchu, City in the Clouds."
Read each statement and then answer the questions. Check your answers before
you begin the reading.

> High in the mountains of Peru, an ancient city hides in the clouds.

1. An *ancient* city is very . . .

   (A) old.
   (B) famous.
   (C) beautiful.

> The ruins of the city sit on a ridge . . .

2. What are *ruins*?

   (A) The remains of old buildings
   (B) Tall towers
   (C) Streets

3. Which of these drawings represents a *ridge*?

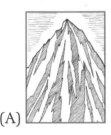
(A)

(B)

(C)

> From below, the city is completely hidden .

4. A city that is *hidden* . . .

   (A) is unsafe.
   (B) cannot be seen.
   (C) can be easily attacked.

Yale University and the National Geographic Society gave him money to return to Peru and remove the trees from the ruins.

5. To *remove* trees means to . . .

(A) plant them in another place.
(B) take them away.
(C) burn them.

The Inca ruled a powerful empire in South America until the Spanish conquered them in the sixteenth century.

6. Another word for *powerful* is . . .

(A) legendary.
(B) strong.
(C) long-lasting.

Archaeologists believe that Machu Picchu was a royal residence built by the Incan king Pachacuti.

7. What job do *archaeologists* do?

(A) Plan and build houses and other buildings
(B) Classify animals and plants
(C) Find and study objects from the past

8. A *residence* is a . . .

(A) home.
(B) fortress for soldiers.
(C) place to keep treasures.

Some tourists hike up the mountain on the Incan Trail.

9. To *hike* is to . . .

(A) ride a bicycle.
(B) ride a horse.
(C) walk.

And because the lost city is so remarkable and the location is so beautiful, it will be difficult to stop people from visiting the City in the Clouds.

10. Another word for *remarkable* is . . .

(A) wonderful.
(B) isolated.
(C) historic.

While You Read

Here are six points that are discussed in the reading. There is one point for each paragraph. While you read, put the points in order from 1 to 6.

_____ The Inca and their reasons for building Machu Picchu
_____ The first outsider visits Machu Picchu
_____ The location of Machu Picchu
_____ Tourism at Machu Picchu
_____ Bingham gets money to return to Machu Picchu
_____ The mystery of Machu Picchu

MACHU PICCHU, CITY IN THE CLOUDS

1 High in the mountains of Peru, an ancient city hides in the clouds. The ruins of the city sit on a ridge between Machu Picchu (Old Mountain) and Huayna Picchu (Young Mountain). Far below, the Urubamba River flows through the forest. From below, the city is hidden. For nearly 450 years, the world did not know Machu Picchu, the City in the Clouds, was there.

2 Outsiders did not visit Machu Picchu until about one hundred years ago. Hiram Bingham, an explorer and a professor from Yale University, was the first to come to the city. Bingham went to Peru to explore in 1909. In 1911, Bingham met Braulio Borda, a man who owned a large farm near Machu Picchu. Borda told Bingham that there were some old buildings covered by the forest in the mountains near his farm. Traveling on

Fig. 11.2 Hiram Bingham.

horseback, Bingham went to Borda's farm. Bingham climbed up to the ridge and there, to his surprise, were the ruins of a lost city.

3   Bingham returned to the United States to tell others about the City in the Clouds. Yale University and the National Geographic Society gave him money to return to Peru and remove the trees from the ruins.

4   Machu Picchu was built by the Inca. The Inca ruled a powerful empire in South America until the Spanish conquered them in the sixteenth century. Archaeologists believe that Machu Picchu was a royal residence built by the Incan king Pachacuti. Machu Picchu was also a religious center that honored the Incan sun god.

5   However, the people of the great Incan city seemed to disappear. What happened to the people of Machu Picchu? That remains a mystery. Around A.D. 1450, Spanish soldiers captured many Incan cities. When the Spanish captured a city, they destroyed the temples. However, the temples at Machu Picchu were not destroyed. One theory is that disease killed the people of Machu Picchu. Another theory is that a group of people called the Antis from the Amazonian jungle attacked and killed the people of the city.

6   Today, Machu Picchu is the most important tourist site in South America. Thousands of tourists visit daily. Most take the train from the nearby city of Cuzco and then take a bus up the

mountain to the ruins. Some tourists hike up the mountain on the Incan Trail. Soon there may be a cable car[1] to bring even more visitors to the site. Archeologists worry that too many tourists will damage the site. However, tourism is important to Peru. And because the lost city is so remarkable and the location is so beautiful, it will be difficult to stop people from visiting the City in the Clouds.

Note

1. A *cable car* travels through the air on strong wires called cables.

After You Read

➤ Understanding the Reading

Answer these multiple-choice questions to see how well you understood the reading.

1. The author does not give the English meaning of . . .

   (A) Machu Picchu.
   (B) Huayna Picchu.
   (C) Urubamba.

2. Where was the city of Machu Picchu built?

   (A) In the forest by a river
   (B) On a ridge between two mountains
   (C) On the top of a mountain peak

3. How long was the city of Machu Picchu hidden?

   (A) 150 years
   (B) 300 years
   (C) 450 years

4. What was Braulio Borda's profession?

   (A) Archaeologist
   (B) Farmer
   (C) Professor

5. Why did Yale University and the National Geographic Society give money to Bingham?

   (A) To remove the trees from the ruins
   (B) To look for another lost city
   (C) To tell others about Machu Picchu

6. Machu Picchu was NOT a . . .

   (A) center of religion.
   (B) home for the Incan king.
   (C) strong military fort.

7. Which of these statements about the people of Machu Picchu is definitely NOT true?

   (A) They were captured by the Spanish.
   (B) They were killed by the Antis.
   (C) They died from a disease.

8. Which of these might be built at Machu Picchu soon?

   (A) A trail for hikers
   (B) A cable car
   (C) A railroad

❯ Vocabulary Building

Fill in the blanks in the sentences below with one of these words from the reading.

| ruins | empire | conquered | residence |
| theory | remarkable | hike | outsider |

1. The scientist is doing an experiment to try to prove his

   _____.

2. Britain was the last province that was _____ by the Romans.

3. A: I plan to _____ to Crystal Lake today.

   B: That's a long walk. Be sure to bring lunch and plenty of water.

4. The Prime Minister of the U.K. has an official _____ at 10 Downing Street in London.

5. Leonardo da Vinci was a _____ man. He could do almost everything.

6. Not much is left today of the old castle. There are only a few stone
   _____.

7. When I first moved to this town, I felt like an _____. Now I
   have made some friends and I feel at home here.

8. At one time the _____ of the Aztecs covered most of central
   Mexico.

Reading Skill: Scanning 2

In Unit 7, you practiced scanning for facts by finding the paragraph that had
certain information. In this unit, you will practice scanning to find the
answers for specific questions.

Remember: When you scan, decide what information you are looking for.
Hold one or two key words in your mind, then quickly look for this
information in the article.

Exercise: Working as quickly as possible, try to find the information in the
reading that you need to answer these questions. Write down the answers in the
blanks. Try to finish this exercise in five minutes or less.

Beginning time: _____

1. What country is Machu Picchu in? _____

2. What was the name of the king who built Machu Picchu?

   _____

3. How did Hiram Bingham travel to Braulio Borda's farm?

   _____

4. What does *Huayna Picchu* mean in the Inca language? _____

5. What did the Spanish do when they captured an Incan city?

   _____

6. Where did the Antis come from? _____

7. Where did Hiram Bingham teach? _____

8. What is the name of the trail hikers use to go to Machu Picchu?

   _____

9. When did Hiram Bingham find Machu Picchu? _____

10. What is the name of the river that flows through the forest below Machu Picchu? _____

Ending time: _____

➤ Focus on Listening

Listen to the recording of the reading "Machu Picchu, City in the Clouds." You will hear this reading two times. The first time, read along with the recording. Listen to the sound and tone of the words. The second time, listen for meaning. Do not look at the reading. Try to follow the ideas by listening only.

As you listen the second time, the speaker will stop occasionally and make statements about the reading. Decide if the statements are true or false. Fill in the space of the circled T or F according to what you hear and remember from the reading.

1. Ⓣ Ⓕ   5. Ⓣ Ⓕ

2. Ⓣ Ⓕ   6. Ⓣ Ⓕ

3. Ⓣ Ⓕ   7. Ⓣ Ⓕ

4. Ⓣ Ⓕ   8. Ⓣ Ⓕ

➤ Writing and Discussion Questions

Work with a partner or group to answer these questions.

1. Would you like to visit Machu Picchu? Why or why not?

2. Machu Picchu is Peru's top tourist site. Describe one tourist site in your country or in your region of the world.

3. Machu Picchu is one of the most famous architectural sites in the world. Here is a list of other famous architectural sites. Use the Internet to get basic information about three of these sites. Find out where they are located, when they were built, and other basic facts. Try to find pictures of the sites. Write several sentences about each of the three sites that you choose. Share the information that you find with the class.

Teotihuacan	Chaco Canyon	Prambanan	Tikal
Lo Monthang	Knossos	Palenque	Easter Island
Pompei	Ephesus	Petra	Stonehenge
Sukhotai	Luxor Temple	Angkor Wat	

≫ Crossword Puzzle

Complete the puzzle with words from the reading.

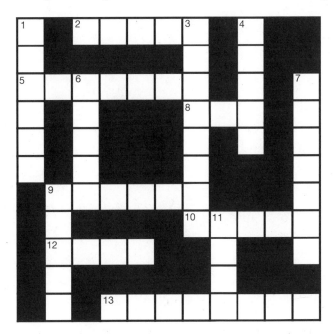

Across

2 Tourists usually come to Machu Picchu on a train from the city of _____.

5 Machu Picchu is an _____ city hidden in the clouds.

8 Machu Picchu was built partly to honor the _____ god.

9 Bingham got money to _____ the trees from Machu Picchu.

10 Machu Picchu is built on a _____ between two mountain peaks.

12 Bingham was a professor at _____ University.

13 The _____ River flows through the forest below Machu Picchu.

Down

1 _____ Picchu means "Young Mountain."

3 Bingham was the first _____ to visit Machu Picchu.

4 The _____ of Machu Picchu were covered with trees.

6 There is a plan to build a _____ car to Machu Picchu.

7 The Spanish destroyed the _____ as soon as they captured an Incan city.

9 Machu Picchu served partly as a _____ residence.

11 The _____ had a powerful empire in South America in the fifteenth century.

Bird Watching in Taiwan

Fig. 12.1 Taiwanese birdwatchers.

Before You Read

❯ Warm-Up Questions

Discuss these questions in pairs or groups. Share your ideas with the class.

1. Look at the picture above, and describe what the people are doing. What is this chapter about?

2. Many people enjoy this popular outdoor hobby. Why do you think this is true?

≫ Vocabulary Preview

These statements come from the reading "Bird Watching in Taiwan." Read each statement and then answer the questions. Check your answers before you begin the reading.

These beautiful black-faced spoonbills are some of the world's rarest birds.

1. This sentence tells us that . . .

   (A) spoonbills are some of the world's biggest birds.
   (B) spoonbills are very smart birds.
   (C) there are very few spoonbills in the world.

Almost immediately , a crowd of people begins to shoot them.

2. If something happens *immediately*, it happens very . . .

   (A) unexpectedly.
   (B) soon after something else happens.
   (C) slowly.

No, the people who have been waiting are happy to see the spoonbills. They are only shooting photographs.

3. Which of these is used to *shoot* photographs?

   (A) A gun
   (B) A pen
   (C) A camera

These people are some of Taiwan's many enthusiastic birdwatchers, or, as they are usually called, birders.

4. If people are *enthusiastic,* they . . .

   (A) have a lot of energy and interest.
   (B) are just beginners.
   (C) have a lot of information and experience.

Birders look at birds at a distance, usually through binoculars .

5. Which of these are *binoculars*?

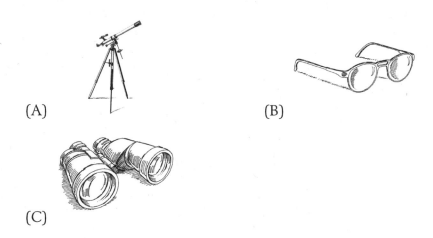

(A)   (B)

(C)

This hobby began in Europe in the 1800s and spread around the world.

6. A *hobby* is an activity people do . . .

(A) at work.
(B) for pleasure.
(C) because they are forced to.

Taiwan is a paradise for birders.

7. A *paradise* is a . . . place

(A) perfect
(B) difficult
(C) strange

This small island has many different climate zones , from tropical on the coast to cold in the mountains. Each of these areas attracts different species.

8. Circle the word that is close in meaning to *zones*.

The plan has been delayed for now, and the population of spoonbills has almost doubled .

9. If a plan has been *delayed*, it . . .

(A) has been slowed down.
(B) is ahead of schedule.
(C) has been completely canceled.

10. If the population has almost *doubled*, it has . . .

    (A) decreased by 50%.
    (B) increased by 100%.
    (C) almost disappeared.

While You Read

Here are seven points that are discussed in the reading. There is one point for each paragraph. While you read, put the points in order from 1 to 7.

_____ Taiwan: a perfect place for bird watching
_____ Birdwatchers help protect Taiwan's birds from development
_____ Taiwan's birdwatchers welcome the spoonbills
_____ Bird watching becomes a popular hobby in Taiwan
_____ Dangers to birds and dangers to human health
_____ The spoonbills return to Taiwan
_____ Wild Bird Society statistics about Taiwan's birds

BIRD WATCHING IN TAIWAN

Fig. 12.2 Black-faced spoonbill.

It is a cloudy day in October. Over the Tseng-wen estuary[1] in Taiwan, a group of large white birds with black faces appears. These beautiful black-faced spoonbills are some of the world's rarest birds. There are only about six hundred of them in the world. The birds have flown all the way from their summer home in Korea. Now, they circle and land. Almost immediately, a crowd of people begins to shoot them.

2   Is this the end for the spoonbills? No, the people who have been waiting are happy to see the spoonbills. They are only shooting photographs. These people are some of Taiwan's enthusiastic birdwatchers, or, as they are usually called, birders.

3   Birders look at birds from a distance, usually through binoculars. This hobby began in Europe in the 1800s and spread around the world. Although it did not come to Taiwan until the 1960s, it has become very popular there, especially among young people. Groups of young birders compete to spot the most species. Why do so many students enjoy birding? It gets them out of the cities and into nature, they explain. "I never knew how beautiful Taiwan was until I started birding," says one young bird watcher. In addition to local birders, there are also many bird watching tourists from North America, Europe, and Japan.

4   Taiwan is a paradise for birders. This small island has many different climate zones, from tropical on the coast to cold in the mountains. Each of these areas attracts different species—about 440 species altogether. For comparison, in the United States, which is over 250 times larger than Taiwan, there are only 800 species. In fact, Taiwan has more species per square kilometer than almost any other place in the world. Only Madagascar has a greater number of species per square kilometer than Taiwan.

5   The Wild Bird Society of Taiwan says that 40% of Taiwan's birds are residents. Resident birds live in Taiwan all the time. Most of them live in the mountains in the middle of the island. Of these, fifteen species are found only in Taiwan, not in any other country. Another 40% are migrants. In other words, they don't live

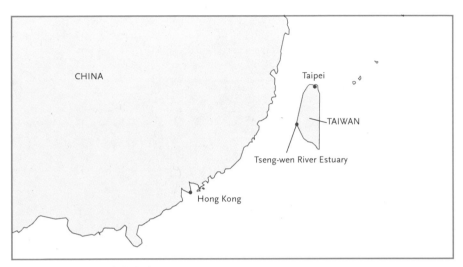

Fig 12.3 Taiwan and the Chinese coast.

in Taiwan all the time. Many birds fly south from Siberia, Korea, and Japan in the fall. Some continue south to Indonesia, the Philippines, Australia, and New Zealand. Others stay in Taiwan. In the spring, Taiwan is visited by birds from the south. The last 20% of Taiwan's birds are, well, lost. They usually stop on the island because of bad weather. These birds are called vagrants.

6   Taiwan's birders love to watch birds, but they also try to protect them. They have had some success. In 1981, the Taiwanese government created special areas for birds. Birders also try to stop industrial development in places where rare birds live. They are fighting against a plan to build an oil refinery[2] and steel mill near the spoonbills' nesting ground[3]. The plan has been delayed for now, and the population of spoonbills has almost doubled.

7   "Today the birds, tomorrow the humans," birders often say. In other words, the same ecological problems that kill birds now may someday endanger people's health. In Taiwan, birders are working to save birds for future generations to enjoy. And thanks

to the birders, the black-faced spoonbills still have a home to come to from their long trip across the sea.

___

Notes

1. An *estuary* is the place where a river grows wide and then enters the sea.

2. An *oil refinery* is a factory for producing gasoline from crude oil.

3. A *nesting ground* is an area where birds build nests and lay eggs.

After You Read

❯ Understanding the Reading

Answer these multiple-choice questions to see how well you understood the reading.

1. Where do the black-faced spoonbills spend their summer?

   (A) In Korea
   (B) In Taiwan
   (C) In Europe

2. When the spoonbills arrive in Taiwan, people try to . . .

   (A) take their pictures.
   (B) capture them.
   (C) shoot them with guns.

3. When did bird watching first come to Taiwan?

   (A) In the 1800s
   (B) In the 1960s
   (C) In the 1990s

4. The author does NOT compare the . . .

   (A) number of bird species in Taiwan and the number of bird species in the U. S.
   (B) number of people in Taiwan and the number of people in the U. S.
   (C) size of Taiwan and the size of the U. S.

5. How many species of birds can be found in Taiwan?

   (A) 250
   (B) 440
   (C) 800

6. Which of these countries has the largest number of bird species per square kilometer?

(A) The United States
(B) Taiwan
(C) Madagascar

7. The smallest percentage of birds in Taiwan are . . .

(A) vagrants.
(B) residents.
(C) migrants.

8. In the spring, birds come to Taiwan mainly from the . . .

(A) west.
(B) north.
(C) south.

➤ Vocabulary Building

Fill in the blanks in the sentences below with one of these words from the reading.

rarest	immediately	hobby	paradise
climate	delayed	species	endanger

1. I didn't write down my ideas _____, and now I've forgotten them.

2. A: Do you have a _____?

   B: Yes, I enjoy fixing up old cars so that they look new again.

3. The _____ in Mongolia in the winter is cold and dry.

4. The Yangtze River dolphin is one of the _____ mammals in the world. There are probably only about fifty of them still living.

5. Switzerland is a _____ for skiers and mountain climbers.

6. Forest fires _____ many animals.

7. There are more _____ of insects than there are of any other kind of animal.

8. My flight to Hong Kong was _____ for four hours because of mechanical problems on the plane.

Reading Skill: Understanding Vocabulary from Context

In Unit 6, you used the words around an unfamiliar word to select the correct definition in a dictionary. When you see a word that you do not know in a reading, you can often use the words and sentences around it—the context—to help you to guess the meaning of the word without using a dictionary. Guessing words from context is a useful skill. It saves you time because you do not need to look up every unfamiliar word in a dictionary. More importantly, it helps you build your vocabulary quickly.

Here are some clues to getting vocabulary from context:

- Look for words that have similar meaning.

- Look for terms that signal the meaning such as "or" or "in other words."

- Look for words in the same word family.

- Look for examples that can explain what type of word it is.

- Think about the topic of the sentence or passage—what it is about.

- Use your general knowledge—of the topic, related words, and parts of the word itself.

Exercise: Read the passage, and use the context to guess the meaning of the highlighted words. Then match these terms with the definitions.

Because of the success of the program to save the black-faced spoonbills, birdwatchers from Taiwan and abroad have been trying to save the habitats of other rare species of birds. One endangered species is the fairy pitta. In Chinese, this lovely little bird is known as the eight-color bird because of its brilliant multicolored feathers. The fairy pitta nests in Taiwan from May to August, then spends the rest of the year in the Philippines. A recent census showed that there were only two thousand fairy pittas still alive. Birders have persuaded the government to block industrial development near the habitat of the fairy pitta in Taiwan. They also want the government to create a sanctuary protecting the pitta permanently.

Another key development in bird watching in Taiwan was the rediscovery of a sea bird called the Chinese crested tern. Birders thought that the crested tern was extinct, but several years ago, one was seen on an uninhabited island off the coast of Taiwan. The global organization Bird Life International sent Richard Thomas, an acclaimed expert in bird watching, to Taiwan to search for more of these rare birds.

_____ 1. abroad   (A) important; vital

_____ 2. brilliant   (B) admired; well-known and liked

_____ 3. census   (C) other countries

_____ 4. persuaded   (D) bright; shining; colorful

_____ 5. sanctuary   (E) without any people

_____ 6. key   (F) a count of people or animals; a survey

_____ 7. uninhabited   (G) convinced; talked into; influenced

_____ 8. acclaimed   (H) a safe place

➤ Focus on Listening

Listen to the recording of the reading "Bird Watching in Taiwan." You will hear this reading two times. The first time, read along with the recording. Listen to the sound and tone of the words. The second time, listen for meaning. Do not look at the reading. Try to follow the ideas by listening only.

As you listen the second time, the speaker will stop occasionally and make statements about the reading. Decide if the statements are true or false. Fill in the space of the circled T or F according to what you hear and remember from the reading.

1. Ⓣ Ⓕ   5. Ⓣ Ⓕ

2. Ⓣ Ⓕ   6. Ⓣ Ⓕ

3. Ⓣ Ⓕ   7. Ⓣ Ⓕ

4. Ⓣ Ⓕ   8. Ⓣ Ⓕ

➤ Writing and Discussion Questions

Work with a partner or group to answer these questions.

1. Do you think you would enjoy bird watching? Why or why not?

2. Describe several popular hobbies in your country. Why do you think they are popular?

3. Do you prefer indoor activities or outdoor activities? Explain your answer.

4. Here are the names of some other endangered species. Use the Internet to learn some basic information about three of them. Find out what kind of animal they are, what country they live in, how many of them are left, and other basic facts about them. Try to find pictures of them. Write several sentences about each of the three species that you choose. Share the information that you learn with the class.

Java rhino	kouprey	golden lion tamarin
giant ibis	coelacanth	riverine rabbit
Komodo dragon	kokako	giant panda

» Crossword Puzzle

Complete the puzzle with words from the reading.

Across

2 Birdwatchers are also called _____.

4 Birdwatchers use _____ to look at birds.

8 Taiwan has a variety of climate _____.

9 The black-faced spoonbill is one of the world's _____ birds.

10 _____ are birds that come to a place by mistake.

Down

1 The _____ of bird watching began in the 1800s in Europe.

3 The number of spoonbills has almost _____ in recent years.

5 Birdwatchers helped protect the spoonbills' _____ ground.

6 There are 440 _____ of birds in Taiwan.

7 Spoonbills spend their summers in _____.

The Last Flight of the Concorde

Fig. 13.1 The Concorde taking off.

Before You Read

❯ Warm-Up Questions

Discuss these questions in pairs or groups. Share your ideas with the class.

1. What do you know about the Concorde? Look at the photograph and describe it. Then tell the class what you have heard or read about this airplane.

2. Look at the photograph again, especially at the airplane's nose. Skim the reading to find out why the nose points down.

❯ Vocabulary Preview

These statements come from the reading "The Last Flight of the Concorde." Read each statement and then answer the questions. Check your answers before you begin the reading.

The fastest, highest-flying, most elegant airplane in the world: That is how many passengers described the Concorde.

1. *Elegant* means . . .

(A) beautiful in a stylish way.
(B) easy to operate.
(C) expensive.

The Concorde was a joint project of a British and a French aircraft company.

2. A *joint* project . . .

(A) is a cooperative project.
(B) takes a long time to complete.
(C) is very successful.

When it took off or landed, its needle -shaped nose pointed downwards so that the pilots could see the ground in front of them.

3. Which of these is a *needle*?

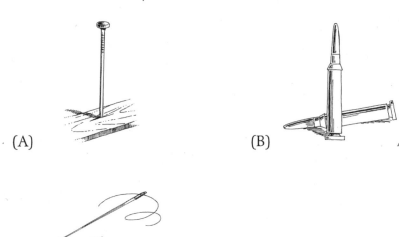

(A)

(B)

(C)

This made the Concorde look like a bird of prey .

4. A *bird of prey* is a bird that . . .

   (A) hunts animals or other birds.
   (B) flies very fast.
   (C) has a long, thin body.

The British and French designers had high hopes for the sleek aircraft.

5. Which of these is a *sleek* vehicle?

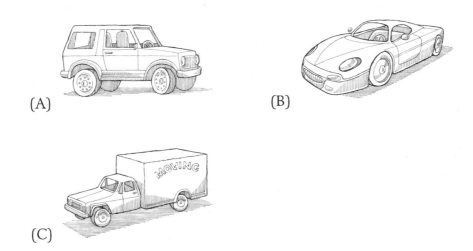

(A)   (B)

(C)

Still another problem was the Concorde's short range .

6. An airplane's *range* is . . .

   (A) the distance it can travel at one time.
   (B) its length from nose to tail.
   (C) the size of its wings.

The plane hit a piece of metal on the ground and the plane caught on fire as it took off.

7. A plane that *caught on fire* is one that began to . . .

   (A) fall.
   (B) travel faster.
   (C) burn.

During this time, the planes were modified to make them safer.

8. *Modified* means . . .

    (A) retired.
    (B) changed.
    (C) produced.

When the Concorde began to fly again, the airline industry was in a slump .

9. When a business is in a *slump*, it . . .

    (A) is profitable.
    (B) has financial problems.
    (C) is at its highest point.

For those who loved this extraordinary airplane, it was the end of an era .

10. An *era* is a . . .

    (A) vehicle.
    (B) story.
    (C) period of time.

While You Read

Here are eight points that are discussed in the reading passage. There is one point for each paragraph. While you read, put the points in order from 1 to 8.

_____ Why the Concorde didn't sell more widely
_____ The Concorde in the 1960s and 1970s
_____ The designers' hopes for the Concorde
_____ Passengers' description of the Concorde
_____ The cost of flying on the Concorde
_____ The end of the Concorde era
_____ The Concorde's safety record
_____ Speed, height, and a special feature

THE LAST FLIGHT OF THE CONCORDE

1   The fastest, highest-flying, most elegant airplane in the world: That is how many passengers described the Concorde. And that's why many passengers were sad when the Concorde flew for the last time.

2   The Concorde was a joint project of a British and a French aircraft company. The companies began designing the plane in 1962. The Concorde's first test flight was in 1969. Its first passenger flight was in 1973.

3   People all over the world loved the Concorde. The world's only supersonic passenger jet, the Concorde flew at twice the speed of sound.[1] Passengers could travel from London to New York in three and half hours. On a 747,[2] this trip takes seven or eight hours. The plane also flew very high, over 18 kilometers high. Passengers could see 747s in the clouds many miles below them. Like astronauts, passengers could even see the round curve of the Earth. And the Concorde had an unusual feature. When it took off or landed, its needle-shaped nose pointed downwards so that the pilots could see the ground in front of them. This made the Concorde look like a bird of prey.

Fig. 13.2 Interior of the Concorde.

4   The British and French designers had high hopes for the sleek aircraft. They wanted to sell hundreds of

them around the world. However, the only airlines that bought and flew the Concorde were British Airways and Air France, and they bought only seven Concordes each. The only regular flights were from Paris and from London to New York. In the winter, there was also a weekly flight from London to Barbados.

5   The Concorde did not sell well because it had a number of problems. The biggest problem was the jet's sonic boom.[3] From the ground, the boom was as loud as thunder. Because of the noise, the Concorde could usually fly only over the ocean, and only a few airports around the world allowed it to land. A second problem was fuel use. The Concorde burned 360 liters of fuel per minute. A 747 uses only about 220. Still another problem was the Concorde's short range. It could fly only about 7,000 kilometers without refueling. Finally, because of its narrow shape, the Concorde could carry only 100 passengers.

6   Because of its limited size, a trip on a Concorde was expensive. Typically, a roundtrip London to New York ticket cost about $7,500—about 20% more than a first-class ticket on a 747. Although tickets were costly, the Concorde was popular with many passengers and both the British and French airlines made a profit on the Concorde until 2000.

7   The Concorde was one of the safest planes of all time—at least, until 2000. In that year, a Concorde crashed at Charles de Gaulle Airport near Paris. The plane hit a piece of metal on the ground and the plane caught on fire as it took off. All 109 people on board and several people on the ground were killed. After the

crash, the Concorde was not allowed to fly for over a year. During this time, the planes were modified to make them safer.

8   When the Concorde began to fly again, the airline industry was in a slump. Few passengers bought tickets. Air France stopped flying the Concorde in May of 2003, and British Airways stopped in October of that year. After the last flight, the remaining Concordes went to museums around the world. For those who loved this extraordinary airplane, it was the end of an era.

Notes

1. At the altitude where the Concorde flew, the *speed of sound* is about 1,060 kilometers an hour.

2. The *747* is an airplane made by the U.S. company Boeing. It is the most commonly used jet for international flights.

3. A *sonic boom* is a loud noise made when a plane flies faster than the speed of sound.

After You Read

➤ Understanding the Reading

Answer these multiple-choice questions to see how well you understood the reading.

1. The Concorde first carried passengers in . . .

   (A) 1962.
   (B) 1969.
   (C) 1973.

2. Which of these comparisons is true?

   (A) The Concorde flies faster than the 747 but not as high.
   (B) The Concorde flies higher than the 747 but not as fast.
   (C) The Concorde flies faster and higher than the 747.

3. Why does the nose of the Concorde sometimes point downwards?

   (A) To give the pilots a clear view
   (B) To lift the Concorde higher into the air
   (C) To increase the speed of the Concorde

4. In total, how many Concordes were sold and flown?

   (A) Seven
   (B) Fourteen
   (C) Hundreds

5. Which of these routes did the Concorde regularly fly?

   (A) London to Paris
   (B) Paris to Barbados
   (C) London to New York

6. What was the Concorde's worst problem?

   (A) Its short range
   (B) Its loud sonic boom
   (C) Its high fuel use

7. How many problems with the Concorde are given in paragraph 5?

   (A) Three
   (B) Four
   (C) Five

8. What happened to the Concordes after Air France and British Airways stopped flying them?

   (A) They were sent to museums.
   (B) They were sold to other airlines.
   (C) They were destroyed.

≫ Vocabulary Building

Fill in the blanks in the sentences below with one of these words or phrases from the reading.

sleek   high hopes   roundtrip   extraordinary
era   slump   caught on fire   birds of prey

Fig. 13.3 A hawk, eagle, and falcon.

1. Do you want a one-way ticket or a _____ one?

2. The museum has an exhibit of furniture from the seventeenth century. There is an exhibit of clothing from that _____ as well.

3. Mr. Van Dorn's business failed because the economy was in a _____.

4. The boat had _____ lines to make it move through the water faster.

5. Eagles, hawks, and falcons are _____.

6. A: What caused the fire in your apartment building?

   B: Someone fell asleep smoking a cigarette and his blankets _____.

7. A: How did your team do in the tournament?

   B: I had _____ that we would win, but we lost the first game.

8. Gloria has an _____ voice. I've never heard anyone sing as well as she does.

Reading Skill: Knowing the Meaning of Prefixes

A *prefix* is a group of letters that comes before the root form of a word. A prefix changes the meaning of words.

Knowing the meaning of prefixes helps you build your vocabulary and learn to guess the meaning of unknown words in a reading, especially if you are familiar with the root.

Here is a list of some of the prefixes used in words in readings in this book. (The number refers to the unit number.)

Prefix	Meaning	Example
pre–	before	predict (1)
re–	again	recharging (1)
mis–	badly, wrongly	mistreats (2)
un–	not	unwrapped (3); unpleasant (5)
inter–	between	international (3)
im–	into	immigrants (4)
ex–	out of, from	exported (5)
dis–	not	disadvantage (6); disappeared (14)
uni–	one	universal (8)
extra–	outside, more than	extraordinary (13)
super–	above, more than	supersonic (13)

Exercise: Match the words on the left with the definitions on the right.

_____ 1. misplace   (A) not normal; strange

_____ 2. predecessor   (B) a large store that sells groceries

_____ 3. expel   (C) put in the wrong place

_____ 4. unusual   (D) make unhappy or upset

_____ 5. displease   (E) begin again

_____ 6. unilateral   (F) bring something into a country

_____ 7. supermarket   (G) someone or something that comes before

_____ 8. extraterrestrial (H) one-sided

_____ 9. restart	(I)	throw out; get rid of
_____ 10. import	(J)	put something between other things
_____ 11. interpose	(K)	from another world

➤ Focus on Listening

Listen to the recording of the reading "The Last Flight of the Concorde." You will hear this reading two times. The first time, read along with the recording. Listen to the sound and tone of the words. The second time, listen for meaning. Do not look at the reading. Try to follow the ideas by listening only.

As you listen the second time, the speaker will stop occasionally and make statements about the reading. Decide if the statements are true or false. Fill in the space of the circled T or F according to what you hear and remember from the reading.

1. Ⓣ Ⓕ   5. Ⓣ Ⓕ

2. Ⓣ Ⓕ   6. Ⓣ Ⓕ

3. Ⓣ Ⓕ   7. Ⓣ Ⓕ

4. Ⓣ Ⓕ   8. Ⓣ Ⓕ

➤ Writing and Discussion Questions

Work with a partner or group to answer these questions.

1. A trip on the Concorde was very expensive. Why do you think people paid so much money to travel on the Concorde? Would you pay $7,500 to fly on the Concorde, or another airplane? Explain.

2. Should the Concorde have continued to fly? Why or why or not?

3. In 1969, the Concorde became the first plane to carry passengers faster than the speed of sound. Here is a list of other "firsts" in the history of airplanes. Find information about two of these on the Internet. (You can use the key words "aviation firsts.") Find out when and where the event happened and other basic information. Write several sentences about each event. Share the information that you find with the class.

1st powered flight	1st helicopter flight	1st jet airliner flight
1st air show	1st commercial airliner	1st in-flight movies
1st transcontinental flight	1st transpacific flight	1st female airline pilot
1st airmail	1st flight attendants	1st non-stop global flight
1st transatlantic flight	1st supersonic flight	1st international air service

» Crossword Puzzle

Complete the puzzle with words from the reading.

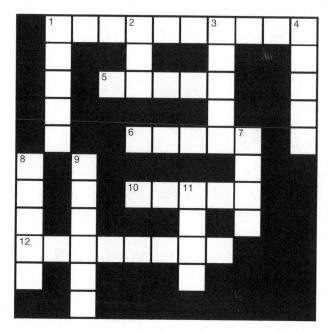

Across

1 The Concorde was the world's only _____ passenger jet.

5 The Concorde's _____ was 7,000 kilometers.

6 Building the Concorde was a _____ British-French project.

10 The designers of the Concorde had high _____ for the plane.

12 After the accident, the Concorde was _____ to make it safer.

Down

1 The Concorde had a very _____ shape.

2 When the last Concorde flew, it was the end of an _____.

3 The Concorde had to fly mainly over the _____.

4 Concorde passengers could see the _____ of the Earth.

7 The first _____ flight of the Concorde was in 1969.

8 When the Concorde began to fly again, the airline industry was in a _____.

9 The Concorde has a _____- shaped nose.

11 The Concorde looks like a bird of _____.

The Legend of Nessie

Fig. 14.1 Artist's rendition of the Loch Ness Monster.

Before You Read

» Warm-Up Questions

Discuss these questions in pairs or groups. Share your ideas with the class.

1. Have you ever heard of the Loch Ness Monster? If so, what do you know about this monster?

2. What is a legend? What other legends do you know about?

➤ Vocabulary Preview

These statements come from the reading "The Legend of Nessie." Read each statement and then answer the questions. Check your answers before you begin the reading.

On the road in front of them, there was a strange creature. The monster was about 10 meters long.

1. Circle the phrase that is close in meaning to *monster*.

In a few moments, the creature disappeared into the lake.

2. If a creature *disappears*, it . . .

    (A) cannot be seen anymore.
    (B) swims in circles.
    (C) attacks.

The Spicers' sighting is only one of about three thousand sightings of "Nessie," the famous monster of the Loch Ness.

3. A *sighting* occurs when someone . . .

    (A) takes a photograph.
    (B) sees something.
    (C) tells a story.

In short , it is the ideal place for a monster to hide.

4. Another way to say *in short* is . . .

    (A) in my opinion.
    (B) briefly.
    (C) for example.

5. An *ideal* place is a . . . place.

    (A) perfect
    (B) secret
    (C) difficult

The U.K. was filled with "Nessie Mania ."

6. What is *mania*?

    (A) A fear of something that is unknown
    (B) A dislike of something for no reason
    (C) A sudden, strong interest in something

Was it a hoax ? Sixty years later, a man named Christian Spurning said that, in fact, it was a hoax.

7. A *hoax* is a . . .

   (A) true story.
   (B) mistake.
   (C) plan to trick people.

Spurning said that he had made a model of Nessie, put it on a toy submarine, and floated it on Loch Ness.

8. A *model* is a . . .of something.

   (A) small copy
   (B) picture
   (C) new idea

9. If you *float* something on a lake, you put it . . . the water.

   (A) under
   (B) on the surface of
   (C) in the air above

Some of these people think that Nessie is a plesiosaur, a dinosaur with a curved neck.

10. Which of these animals has a *curved* neck?

(A)

(B)

(C)

While You Read

Here are eight points that are discussed in the reading. There is one point for each paragraph. While you read, put the points in order from 1 to 8.

_____ Why scientists do not believe in Nessie
_____ Colonel Wilson's photograph: A famous hoax
_____ A description of Loch Ness
_____ The Spicers spot a monster
_____ Tourists and webcams search for Nessie
_____ What some people think Nessie might be
_____ Nessie's "footprints": Another hoax
_____ Nessie Mania in the 1930s

THE LEGEND OF NESSIE

1

Fig. 14.2 Loch Ness.

On July 22, 1933, Mr. and Mrs. Spicer were driving home to London from Scotland. Suddenly, near a lake, Mr. Spicer had to stop their car. On the road in front of them, there was a strange creature. The monster was about 10 meters long. It had grey skin like an elephant and a long neck like a giraffe. In a few moments, the creature disappeared into the lake.

2 The Spicers' sighting is only one of about three thousand sightings of "Nessie," the famous monster of the Loch Ness. Loch Ness in Scotland is the largest lake in the British Isles. It is 38

Fig. 14.3 The Wilson photograph of Nessie in Loch Ness.

kilometers long and about 2.4 kilometers wide. Its average depth is 135 meters, but in places it is much deeper. Its water is cold and dark. In short, it is the ideal place for a monster to hide.

3   There have been many sightings of Nessie over the years. The number of sightings increased when a road around the lake was built in 1933. There were over fifty sightings—including the Spicers'—during 1933. Newspapers wrote about the sightings. The U.K. was filled with "Nessie Mania." The owner of a circus offered £20,000[1] to anyone who could capture the monster. A businessman paid twenty men to watch the lake day and night.

4   In 1934, Nessie was captured—on film. A long-necked monster was photographed swimming in the lake. Colonel Robert Wilson, an army doctor, said that he took the now-famous photo. Was it a hoax? Sixty years later, a man named Christian Spurning said that, in fact, it was a hoax. Spurning said that he had made a model of Nessie, put it on a toy submarine, and floated it on Loch Ness. He photographed the model and gave the picture to Colonel Wilson. Wilson gave it to the newspapers.

5   One year later, a newspaper hired an explorer and hunter named Marmaduke Wetherell to investigate Nessie. Wetherell found some strange footprints near Loch Ness. The Natural History Museum of London investigated. The footprints, too,

were a hoax. Someone had used a hippopotamus foot to make the footprints.

6   You may not be surprised to learn that many scientists do not believe in Nessie. One reason is food supply. Scientists believe that there could not be only one Nessie; there must be a family of Nessies. They say that there is not enough food in or near Loch Ness to feed a family of monsters. Scientists also say that scientific teams have searched Loch Ness again and again. None of these teams has found any sign of Nessie.

7   People who believe in Nessie don't care what the scientists say. Some of these people think that Nessie is a plesiosaur, a dinosaur with a curved neck. This creature has been extinct for 65 million years. Is it possible that a few survived in Loch Ness? Other people think the creature is a very large example of a familiar animal. Maybe Nessie is a giant otter[2] or a huge eel. [3]

8   Loch Ness is one of the top tourist locations in Scotland. Thousands of tourists come to look for the monster. For "Nessie-watchers" who cannot go to Scotland, several webcams[4] show the lake online. You can watch for Nessie yourself while you sit at your home computer.

Notes

1. In 1933, twenty thousand British pounds (£20,000), was the equivalent of over a million U.S. dollars today.

2. The *otter* is a mammal that lives in the water.

3. The *eel* is a kind of fish that looks like a snake.

4. A *webcam* is a camera that sends pictures or video to the Internet.

After You Read

❯ Understanding the Reading

Answer these multiple-choice questions to see how well you understood the reading.

1. The color of the monster's skin is compared to that of . . . .

   (A) a hippopotamus.
   (B) an elephant.
   (C) a giraffe.

2. How many total sightings have there been of the Loch Ness Monster?

   (A) Around 50
   (B) Around 150
   (C) Around 3,000

3. Which of these statements about Loch Ness is NOT true?

   (A) It is shallow and very wide.
   (B) It is long but not very wide.
   (C) It is cold and dark.

4. When did the world learn that the Wilson photograph was a hoax?

   (A) In 1934
   (B) In 1964
   (C) In 1994

5. What did Wilson do?

   (A) He built a model and put it on the toy submarine.
   (B) He took a photograph of the model.
   (C) He sent the photograph to the newspapers.

6. Which of these hired Marmaduke Wetherell to investigate Nessie?

   (A) A museum
   (B) A newspaper
   (C) A circus

7. How many reasons does the author give to explain why scientists don't believe in Nessie?

(A) One
(B) Two
(C) Three

8. No one thinks that Nessie is really . . .

(A) an elephant.
(B) a large eel.
(C) a dinosaur.

» Vocabulary Building

Fill in the blanks in the sentences below with one of these words from the reading.

circus   model   sightings   footprints
creature   floated   ideal   investigated

Fig. 14.4 Clowns and acrobats.

1. The police _____ the crime but did not find the criminal.

2. Jack has a _____ of a sailing ship on his desk.

3. A: What's your favorite act at the _____?

   B: I love the clowns and the acrobats.

4. The blue whale is the largest _____ in the world.

5. In the late 1940s, there were many _____ of UFOs, or flying saucers.

6. There was an animal near my house sometime during the night. In the morning, I saw its _____ in the snow.

7. Betina _____ on her back in the swimming pool.

8. The sky is blue, the temperature is mild; this is an _____ day for a hike.

Reading Skill: Making Inferences

Information in a reading is usually given directly.

> On July 22, 1933, Mr. and Mrs. Spicer were driving home to London from Scotland.

The statement tells us clearly that an action happened, who acted, and when and where the action occurred.

However, the author commonly *implies* information about a subject, action, or object, and the reader *infers*, or *makes an inference* about it.

> The average depth of Loch Ness is 135 meters, but in places, it is much deeper.

This sentence also clearly states a fact. However, the writer *implies* another fact, and the reader can *infer* it: the depth varies. Loch Ness is deep in some places and shallow in other places. The clues to the inference are the words "average" and "in places."

Writers commonly imply their points. Readers piece information together and draw conclusions. By practicing this key skill, you will learn to *read between the lines*. You will also become a much more skillful reader.

Exercise: Here are some statements related to the reading. Read each statement and the inference that follows. Put an **I** in the blank if the inference is correct; put an **X** if it is not.

Some researchers think that Nessie is a giant mammal, not a large reptile. Large reptiles usually live in warm, tropical waters.

_____ 1. Giant mammals can live in cold water.

Today, more and more people visit Loch Ness, and most of them carry cameras.

_____ 2. Today, more and more people take pictures of the Loch Ness monster.

Recently, some deep underwater caves were found at the bottom of Loch Ness. Some people think that these caves explain why scientific teams are not able to locate the Loch Ness monster.

_____ 3. Some people think that the monster hides in the caves.

Before 1933, most of the visitors to Loch Ness went there to fish and relax, not to look for the monster.

_____ 4. After 1933, most people went to Loch Ness to look for the monster.

Many of the people who say they have seen the Loch Ness Monster describe the monster very differently. In fact, it sounds as if they are describing dozens of different animals.

_____ 5. There are probably many different monsters living in Loch Ness.

Professor Kettle is a well-known Loch Ness monster hunter. However, he doesn't look like one because he doesn't have a beard.

_____ 6. Most Loch Ness monster hunters have beards.

➤ Focus on Listening

Listen to the recording of the reading "The Legend of Nessie." You will hear this reading two times. The first time, read along with the recording. Listen to the sound and tone of the words. The second time, listen for meaning. Do not look at the reading. Try to follow the ideas by listening only.

As you listen the second time, the speaker will stop occasionally and make statements about the reading. Decide if the statements are true or false. Fill in the space of the circled T or F according to what you hear and remember from the reading.

1. Ⓣ Ⓕ   5. Ⓣ Ⓕ

2. Ⓣ Ⓕ   6. Ⓣ Ⓕ

3. Ⓣ Ⓕ   7. Ⓣ Ⓕ

4. Ⓣ Ⓕ   8. Ⓣ Ⓕ

❯ Writing and Discussion Questions

Work with a partner or group to answer these questions.

1. Is there really a Loch Ness monster? Explain your opinion. Base your answer on information in the reading.

2. Loch Ness is one of the top tourist locations in Scotland. Would you like to visit Loch Ness? Why or why not?

 3. There are many other stories of monsters that live in lakes. Here is a list of lakes that are believed to have monsters. Use the Internet to try to get some basic information about three of these lakes. Find out what country the lake is in, what the name or nickname of the monster is, and other basic facts about the monster. If possible, find a picture of the monster or the lake. Write several sentences about each of the lakes that you choose. Share the information that you learn with the class.

Flathead Lake	Lake Champlain	Lake Tianchi
Lagerfljót	Hamilton Lake	Lake Brosno
Lake Ikeda	Lake Manitoba	Lake Okanagan
Lake Storsjon	Lake Van	Lake Kokkol
Nahuel Huapi Lake	Lake Tele	Silver Lake

» Crossword Puzzle

Complete the puzzle with words from the reading.

Across

5 Mr. and Mrs. _____ saw a strange creature in 1933.

6 The owner of a _____ offered money for the capture of the monster.

9 Marmaduke Wetherell was an explorer and a _____.

10 You can look for the Loch Ness monster on line through several _____.

Down

1 In 1933, "Nessie _____" swept through the U.K.

2 The Loch Ness monster's nickname is _____.

3 Loch Ness is the _____ place for a monster to hide.

4 There have been over three thousand _____ of the Loch Ness monster.

7 The Wilson photograph shows a monster with a _____ neck.

8 Some people think the monster is a large _____ or an eel.

9 The footprints around the lake were a _____.

Vocabulary Index

Reading Skills Chart

Reading Skill	Unit Section	Page Number
Comprehension (general)	Understanding the Reading:	
	While You Read	4, 16, 28, 41, 53, 64, 76, 87, 98, 112, 125, 135, 146, 158
	After You Read	6, 18, 31, 43, 56, 66, 79, 89, 101, 114, 127, 138, 149, 161

Inferences
   infer
   imply
   make an inference
	Reading Skills	163-64

Main Ideas
   summary sentences
   thesis statements
   topic sentences
	Reading Skills	8-10

Main Ideas and Details	Reading Skills	58
Meaning of Words	Reading Skills	68-70

Phrasal Verbs
   blow up
   cut off
   depends on
   died out
   heading for
   in favor of
   knocked down
	Reading Skills	117-19

Reading Skill	Unit Section	Page Number
Verbs 　meaning of 　present perfect tense 　simple past tense 　simple present tense	Reading Skills	21-22
Vocabulary from Context 　related words 　similar words	Reading Skills	140-41
Vocabulary Words	Vocabulary Previews Vocabulary Building	2, 14, 26, 39, 51, 62, 74, 85, 96, 110, 123, 133, 144, 156 7, 20, 33, 45, 57, 67, 80, 91, 103, 116, 128, 139, 151, 162
Word Families 　antonyms 　dictionaries 　synonyms 　thesaurus	Reading Skills	104-6